# NOTES FROM A MAINE KITCHEN

# NOTES
## from a
# Maine Kitchen

### Seasonally Inspired
### Recipes

*by*

KATHY GUNST

ISBN: 978-0-892-72917-3

Library of Congress
Cataloging-in-Publication Data

Gunst, Kathy.
  Notes from a Maine kitchen : seasonally inspired recipes / by Kathy Gunst.
     p. cm.
  Includes index.
  ISBN 978-0-89272-917-3
1.  Cooking, American—New England style. 2.  Cooking—Maine.
3.  Seasonal cooking. 4.  Cookbooks.  I. Title.
  TX715.2.N48G86 2011
  641.59741--dc23
                    2011015397

Front Cover Design by Miroslaw Jurek
Interior Design by Jennifer Baum

Cover and author photograph by Stacey Cramp
Illustrations by Patrick Corrigan

Set in Esta.
Printed in China

5         4         3         2         1

**Down East**
Books • Magazine • Online
www.downeast.com
Distributed to the trade
by National Book Network

To Nancy and Lee Gunst,
who first brought me to Maine

# ACKNOWLEDGEMENTS ❧

Living in a place like Maine means relying on people. When there's a freak blizzard in January and you need a roof rake, neighbors are there. When you need someone to walk the dog, friends volunteer. When you need an extra maple syrup bucket for tapping your trees, or a cup of sugar, sea salt, or olive oil, friends and neighbors have always been there for me. I live in that kind of place.

Thanks to Hope Murphy for helping me test recipes, tasting everything so critically, and being such a good friend. To Karen Frillmann for being there, urging me to go "deeper," and sending me off in the right direction when I get lost. To Elisa Newman, who listened to every single word and retested the baked goods so accurately. Thanks to Valerie Jorgensen, Jess Thomson, Grace Young, Brad Laslett, Allison Clark, and Galen Mott. And to the talented women in my writers group, for all their editing and encouragement: Marie Harris, Susan Poulin, Tess Feltes, Pat Spalding, Mimi White. And to those who have taught me to shape words: Pam Houston, Fenton Johnson, Nancy Aronie. And thanks to the IACP for making the trip to the White House happen.

Many thanks to chefs Sam Hayward and Rob Evans, the entire board (past and present) of Share our Strength Southern Maine. And to all those who grow and raise food in Maine, for their hard work and extraordinary dedication.

To the Down East family. Special thanks to Lorie Costigan, who first invited me to write my blog, *Notes from a Maine Kitchen* (www.downeast.com/blogs/notesfromamainekitchen), and to Kathleen Fleury, my editor, for her careful reading, skillful edits, and encouragement. Thanks to John Viehman for his patience. Many thanks to Patrick Corrigan for the beautiful line drawings and to Stacey Cramp for the photograph of the bowl of cranberries on the cover and my author photo.

Special thanks to my agent, Doe Coover, for hanging in there and helping me realize a dream with this book.

To my mother-in-law, Nancy, for her love. To Maya and Emma, my Maine girls, who make everything I do worth doing. To Chloe, my faithful yellow Lab, for getting me away from the computer and into the woods every day. And finally, to John, my editor, my best friend, my love. Thank you.

# CONTENTS

# CONTENTS

# INTRODUCTION ≍

**M**aine has been my home since the early 1980s (which means, no matter how long I live here, I will never be considered a "native"). In December of 1982, I left my job as a magazine editor in New York City, and, John, my boyfriend (who later became my husband at a clambake wedding in the field behind our house) and I moved to an old farmhouse in a small town in southern Maine. (The closet in our first rental house was almost as big as our whole Manhattan apartment!)

We had decided to spend a year in Maine. I would write my first cookbook and John would work as a radio reporter. I remember thinking: Oh, a whole year in Maine! Like a year in Provence, or Tuscany, or Paris. It would be our little adventure, a year away, a time to experience New England.

That first cold winter we would wake up each morning and struggle to light a fire in the woodstove (New York City doesn't provide much training for properly lighting woodstoves). As the cast iron began to heat up and we watched the snow drifts outside, we would often ask each other, "What are we doing here?" And every time we had one of those "Wow-we-made-a-BIG-mistake-moving-to-Maine-in-the-dead-of-winter" days, we would go out and buy lobster. When all else failed, it was lobster that kept us going. Lobster equals Maine and lobsters were a known entity. They were delicious and made us feel so much better about being here. We would buy the largest lobsters we could afford, and marvel at how cheap they were (in those days they really were cheap, particularly in comparison to New York City prices) and steam them and dip the meat into butter and between mouthfuls say to each other, "This is why we moved to Maine." And for a short while, with bellies full of sweet, briny lobster meat, we were just fine. But it got dark at four in the afternoon and temperatures dropped to near zero, and the holidays crept up with our families hundreds of miles away, and again we asked ourselves: "What in hell have we done?"

I first visited Maine as a young child. My grandparents rented a cottage on Kezar Lake in Center Lovell and my parents took us to visit every summer. When I got older, my parents sent me off to a Maine "sleep-away camp." Both of these camps remind me of a time and place that made me feel — calm. I still feel that way living in Maine. I can leave my house unlocked and the keys to my car on the dashboard and wake up to find my car still in the driveway. Maine is a place of extreme beauty; there are hundreds of acres of woods nearby for dog walks, mushroom hunts, and quiet hikes.

The sense of serenity I get from living in Maine has not changed over the years. Neither has the strong sense that this is a place where people really care about community, about one another, and about maintaining a quality of life that is fading fast in America.

One thing that has changed in the past three decades is the food, and mostly for the better. When we first moved here, the food scene was quaint, charming, one might say "old-fashioned." We went to clambakes and lobster boils, church suppers, bean-hole bean suppers, chowder festivals, and many, many potlucks dinners. So long as you liked seafood, things were good. Virtually everything that was delicious about Maine food came from the icy-cold Atlantic.

These days Maine is a major culinary destination, and not only because of lobster. While this is not a book about restaurants or chefs, what inspired me to write this book is how the climate of the food world here has changed dramatically. The local, sustainable food movement is alive and strong, making Maine a place where good local food abounds. Be it wild ramps or fiddleheads, amazing cheeses, crusty breads, smoked local salmon, Maine-grown wheat, berries, and so much more.

The idea for *Notes from a Maine Kitchen* came about when I started writing a blog of the same name for *Down East* magazine at www.DownEast.com. I was interested in exploring the food world in Maine throughout the seasons, from my kitchen and garden and its surroundings. It's been several years of discovering great food, meeting inspiring chefs, gardeners, farmers, and people passionate about making Maine food something worth talking about.

—*Kathy Gunst*

# January

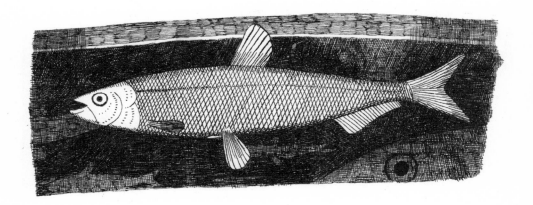

# A WINTER ADVENTURE ON THE CATHANCE RIVER

Truth be told: the idea of sitting in a shack on top of the ice with a hole cut in it, putting slimy bait on a hook, trying to catch smelts has always struck me as a little crazy.

But here I am, just before 8 A.M. on a cold January morning outside Jim McPherson's Smelt Camps in Bowdoinham, Maine. I'm with Sam Hayward, chef of Fore Street restaurant in Portland, and Sam's old friend and fishing buddy, Brett Zachau. It's prime season for smelting, and we're hoping the tide is right and the fish are biting. For me this is a first. I've caught a flounder or two, but I've never fished for smelts, and certainly never stepped inside a smelt camp. I've come hoping to be proven wrong about this whole winter ice fishing thing.

By the time we check in with McPherson and grab our gear from the car — a thermos of coffee, some pastry, a knife, cutting board, worms, and a few kitchen towels — there's a line forming outside the camp office. The Cathance River in Bowdoinham is known as a good fishing spot and a small group of men wait in the cold to sign up for one of McPherson's fishing shacks. I appear to be the only woman for miles around. Although dressed in my three layers of clothing, which makes me very closely resemble the Michelin (wo)man, it's hard to tell what gender I am.

Like the tiny silver fish they are here to catch, these men are drawn by the tide. The best smelt fishing takes place during the incoming tide, which lasts about five or six hours, and on this icy blue morning begins around 8 A.M.

We walk down a plank to the frozen river. I spot water flowing in the center of the river, not more than one hundred feet from where we are standing. Jim McPherson has been running the camps for more than thirty winters, so I'm guessing that if it were unsafe he'd be the first to know. We spot a four-wheeler with a strange-looking building on wheels hitched to the back. Sam and Brent start laughing as McPherson describes the rig: "This is the trailer I used to haul my four-wheelers, but now I use my four-wheeler to haul it. I put a small building on it with a propane heater to keep people warm while I take them upriver. Hop in and we'll get started."

We settle onto little wooden benches built into the side of the shack. I stare out the one small, foggy window in the rear of the building and watch civilization disappear. First the bridge, then the car, the church steeple, and finally the town fades as we drive two miles upriver to a spot called Town Farm Turn, where locals have been fishing for more than a hundred years. It's dead quiet as we step out and set eyes on our camp.

"This here's my deluxe camp. Come on in and I'll show you around," says McPherson, waving his arm at the tiny structure like a game show host displaying a new car we just won. The camp, green with a red door and yellow trim, measures ten feet by ten feet, the size of a large outhouse. Sam and Brent seem awfully impressed. "Wow!" they say in unison. "Look at this. Sixteen lines! Oh boy, we're gonna catch some fish!" I look at these two middle-aged men, one a famous chef and the other a carpenter/builder, and see them as the boys they must have been, gleeful children playing hooky from school on a cold January morning, out on the river, not a worry in the world.

Inside the camp is a small, old, black cast-iron woodstove. There's a pile of wood and McPherson, as part of the fee for renting the camp, has cranked the fire and gotten the place toasty warm. I look down at my hands wrapped inside expedition-style gloves, big, thick things with so much insulation I could probably stick my hand into the icy water and not feel the cold. My whole body starts to sweat.

There's a narrow wooden table and a few fold-up wooden chairs. On either side of the camp McPherson has cut a long, thin rectangle in the ice (what he calls "the race holes") where under foot-thick ice we can see the black water swirl beneath us. At the beginning of the season, sometime near Christmas, he uses a chainsaw to cut out the holes. As long as the camp is in use the ice doesn't have a chance to refreeze completely. McPherson heads upriver every day around 6 A.M. and uses an ice chisel and a skimmer to break up the frozen water so it will be clear by the time the early-morning customers show up. Attached to opposite walls of the camp, above the swirling water, are eight lines dangling over the race holes. The fishing lines end with a hook and a two-ounce lead weight or "sinker" dangling from it.

Brent and Sam start cutting up sand worms, our bait. They're nasty looking and are said to bite. Even after they're cut into 1/4-inch pieces the worms wiggle on the wooden cutting board. We place the bait on the hooks; it's not nearly as hard as it seems once I get the hang of it and forget about the slimy, warm blood coating my fingers.

We drop the lines until they hit the bottom of the river; it takes a while to feel the gentle thud on the muddy riverbed. Then I'm told to raise the line up off the bottom about six to eight inches, and wait.

The woodstove is cranking, and I sit down next to the lines I have baited, expecting to settle in for the long haul. Within seconds (I am prone to exaggeration, but I swear it was only seconds) one of my lines wiggles back and forth. Hate to admit it, but I make a sound like a squeal. "I GOT ONE!" Brent joins in: "Yup! I think you got somethin' there. Give it a quick jerk and pull it up." There, at the end of my line, is a gorgeous eight-inch silver smelt. Before I can pull the fish off the C-shaped hook and rebait it, lines two and five are squiggling. Suddenly things are out of control. We can't bait the lines fast enough.

"We have hit pay dirt," Brent says, slapping his knee. He and Sam are marveling at the situation. "This is the best spot on the river," they say. "Can you even imagine a more perfect spot?" they ask each other, huge grins on their faces. "This is just unreal. Unbelievable."

Within an hour we have almost filled half of a large plastic bucket with more than one hundred smelts. They range in size from tiny ones — about five inches — to really impressive-looking larger ones measuring around nine inches. The smelts have a silvery sheen and when you look at them closely they have a series of bright colors flashing just beneath their skin. "We don't call them rainbow smelts for nothing," says Brent. He explains that smelts are anadromous, a new word for me. It means that smelts, like salmon, live primarily in the ocean, but breed in fresh water.

We drink coffee, stoke the woodstove, and rebait the lines as fast as we can. And then, after about an hour, all activity slows down and the bites stop cold. It's as if we've caught every smelt in the river.

**B**rent Zachau grew up in Bowdoinham, with Jimmy McPherson, and spent much of his childhood right here on the Cathance River, fishing for smelts during the wintertime. He's got a white-gray beard, a baseball cap on his head, and a thick flannel shirt and jeans. He looks straight out of central casting (We need a Mainer!) and he's got the accent to go with the look. "You gotta watch your lines here," he teaches me, playing with the depth of my hooks. "As the tide comes in, the ice lifts so you have to keep dropping your lines to keep the right depth . . . that's pretty much the only trick. That and just hope for the best."

It's quiet for about fifteen minutes, which gives Brent and Sam time to start talking. They pour more black coffee and tell stories about smelt fishing in the "old days," share rumors about locals coming out here with bottles of strong stuff and women ("some kids around here shouldda been named 'Smeltah!' "). And then there are the tales of local teenagers and the trouble/fun they managed to get into spending a few hours in an ice camp in the dead of winter. Sam says, "Ice shacks and smelt fishing are a rite of passage in Maine." As they talk, we pull up the lines, rebait them with fresh worm goo, and reset them at the proper depth. And suddenly, as if nap time is officially over, the lines start dancing, moving slowly, and then with more momentum until we can barely keep up with them again.

As I look into the almost-full bucket of smelts, I think about the pleasure of eating something fresh, even in January in frozen, snowy Maine.

Sam seems to read my mind. "We should think about quitting time and maybe head back to my house to cook some of these up. There's nothing like a fresh smelt that's only been out of the water an hour or so."

As we drive back to town, Sam remembers glorious moonlit nights skating on this river with his wife. These memories lead to a tale of tragedy, about a dear friend who went under one day when the ice just wasn't thick enough. Brent is quiet. "That was my best friend who went down," he says sadly. "I didn't think I would ever go back out on the ice, but here I am. I'm sure glad we did this."

At Sam's house, just a few miles down the road, I learn how to clean smelts. We start with a good pair of kitchen scissors and a quick snip along the belly, or vent, of the smelt and then work our way up toward the head, revealing the roe in the females and the milt in the males. Most of the smelts are females and their daffodil-yellow roe is put aside so we can fry it up for an extra treat. Once the roe and milt are removed, we snip out the digestive track and the gills. At first it seems like a tricky technique, but within a few minutes I'm working my way through the pile.

Sam mixes flour and coarsely ground cornmeal in a large bowl and seasons it with fresh black pepper and Maine sea salt. He lightly coats the cleaned smelts and their roe in the mixture. A well-worn, black cast-iron skillet is placed over high heat with just a coating of canola oil until it's just short of smoking. The smelts fry up in about a minute on each side. We taste them hot, with a squirt of lemon juice, and I'm wondering if any winter food has ever tasted quite this good.

Raw smelts actually smell a lot like cucumbers and their taste is slightly reminiscent of them as well — fresh and subtle. The flesh is delicate, not at all strong and fatty like a fresh sardine or anchovy (which are not, it turns out, related to the smelt). We eat quite a few smelts and try the roe, and then we eat some more.

I ask Sam if he thinks smelts will catch on more due to the recession and tough economic times. "I'm not sure people go after smelts because they're cheap and plentiful," he answers. Sam Hayward is a thinking-man's chef. He knows more about Maine food and its culinary traditions than just about anyone else. "They go after them for their cultural context. Getting outdoors in a smelt camp is a great winter activity when there's nothing else to do. Smelts have a certain panache because of where they are from and how we catch them. They are one of the few fish that have a short season. They are really a delicacy."

As I drive home with a large bag of smelts (we divide up what we haven't eaten between the three of us and there are more than enough for everyone), I have to laugh. Standing on the ice with slimy bait turns out to be a whole lot of fun. Bringing home fresh food in January is even better. You can buy smelts in most fish stores for under four dollars a pound, but getting outside, standing over a hole in the ice, and hanging out with friends makes winter so much sweeter.

17

# Pan-Fried, Cornmeal-Coated Maine Smelts

Find the freshest smelts possible and try them using this simple technique. They are delicious with a simple wedge of lemon, but the Better Than Tartar Sauce *(page 19)* makes for an exceptional meal.

*Serves 4*

> 1 pound fresh smelts
> 1/2 cup flour
> 1/2 cup stone-ground or coarse yellow or white cornmeal
> salt and freshly ground black pepper
> about 3 tablespoons canola or safflower oil
> 1 lemon, cut into wedges
> Better Than Tartar Sauce, *(page 19)*, optional

Lightly rinse the smelts and dry thoroughly.

To clean the smelts: using a small pair of kitchen scissors, hold the smelt belly up in one hand with its head pointing away from you. With the scissors, open the belly by cutting from the vent to the point of the lower jaw. With the back of the thumb of the other hand, push the entrails out of the abdominal cavity in a single motion. Grasp the gills and the entrails and pull them clear of the head. If necessary, use the scissors to cut the esophagus just inside the jaw. Alternately, ask your fish store to clean the smelts for you.

Place the flour, cornmeal, salt, and pepper on a plate and lightly dredge the smelts in the mixture until coated on all sides.

In a large, heavy frying pan (cast iron is ideal), heat the oil over moderately high heat. It's hot enough when you add a speck of the flour mixture and it begins to sizzle. Add the smelts, a few at a time, being careful not to crowd the pan, and cook about 2 to 3 minutes on each side (don't fiddle with the fish — let them cook undisturbed). When you flip the smelts over, they should be golden brown. The timing depends on the size of the fish — a smaller 5-inch smelt will only take about 2 minutes per side and a larger (around 8 or 9 inches long) fish will need to cook closer to 3 minutes per side.

Drain on paper towels and serve hot with lemon wedges and the Better Than Tartar Sauce, if desired.

# Better Than Tartar Sauce

This tartar-like sauce is delicious served with any sautéed or fried fish — smelts, fried clams, sautéed sole or flounder, haddock, etc. You can make it several hours (but not a full day) ahead of time, and cover and refrigerate until ready to serve. The sauce is enough for one pound of fish.

*Makes about 1 cup*

> 1 cup mayonnaise
> 1 small dill or half-sour pickle, finely chopped, plus 1 tablespoon of the liquid
>     or juice from the pickle jar
> 1 scallion, finely chopped
> 1 tablespoon drained capers
> juice of 1/2 large lemon, about 2 tablespoons
> 1 or 2 dashes hot pepper sauce
> salt and freshly ground black pepper
> 2 tablespoons finely chopped parsley

In a small bowl, mix all the ingredients until fully incorporated. Taste for seasoning and add more salt, pepper, or hot sauce to taste. Cover and refrigerate until ready to use.

19

# A STEW FOR A LONG, SLOW MONTH

When it's two below zero, daylight ends around 4 in the afternoon, and the ground is a solid sheet of frozen, slippery ice, I often forget about all the things there are to love about winter. Once the holidays wind down and life resumes its normal beat, I generally dread the long, slow months ahead. But that's the beauty of winter — we get to slow down and focus inward. Inside the house, inside our minds (or what's left of them after the holiday parties and all that rich food and napping). There's no garden to tend, no lawn to mow. And when the sun is shining, and there's a fresh blanket of powder on the fields, there is much to celebrate.

It's not just the slowing down. It's the eating, too. Winter was made for cooking. One night, after the daytime temperature reached a high of 7 degrees and a gray sheet seemed to be tucked into the daytime sky, I spent several hours preparing a chicken stew bathed in red wine, seasoned with bacon, fresh thyme (from my barely surviving kitchen window herb plant), mushrooms, and baby onions (that did survive in our cold, dark basement after being pulled from the garden last September). The stew filled the house with one of those "try to resist me" aromas. It was so intoxicating that when the FedEx guy walked into the mudroom and asked for my signature for a package, he blurted out, "Oh my God, what are you cooking?" And then, only half kidding, "Can I stay for dinner?"

There are few things in this world that smell as good as a slowly simmering stew. Flavors are gently coaxed out of the ingredients. Root vegetables like carrots and onions are asked to release their natural sweetness, while the chicken fills the pot with its meaty essence and huge flavors. It's as if the chicken in this stew is being absorbed by the red wine, taking on its color and flavor, and surrendering any toughness it might have ever had. The bacon provides a meaty backdrop for the stew, and the crimini mushrooms, tasting of bare earth before a snowfall, balance the stew. Local potatoes, peeled and then quartered, are cooked in boiling water and then gently tossed with a little butter and fresh parsley.

Let your food slow down. No quick sautés or throwing a salad together at this time of year. These cold, short days *demand* stews, soups, and braises.

# Parsleyed Potatoes

This is a classic accompaniment to any stew.

*Serves 4*

1½ pounds Maine potatoes, white or yellow fleshed, peeled and quartered
2 tablespoons butter
salt and freshly ground black pepper
¼ cup finely chopped fresh parsley

Bring a medium-size pot of water to a rolling boil over high heat. Add the potatoes, cover, and let cook about 12 to 14 minutes, depending on the variety, or until just tender when pierced in the center with a small, sharp knife. Drain.

Place the potatoes back in the pot and toss gently with the butter, salt, pepper, and parsley. Serve hot.

# Chicken Stew *with* Bacon, Baby Onions, *and* Crimini Mushrooms

This chicken stew, very reminiscent of the classic French *coq au vin*, is best made a day ahead of time, but will work just fine if you cook it a few hours before serving. We had leftover stew for two days and, trust me, it only gets better.

*Serves 4*

2 strips bacon

1½ tablespoons olive oil

1 leek, dark green section discarded, and white and pale green section cut in half lengthwise and then into 1-inch pieces

4 scallions, ends trimmed and cut into ½-inch pieces

12 pearl onions, peeled and left whole, or 4 medium sweet onions, peeled and quartered

2 large carrots, peeled and cut on the diagonal into 1-inch pieces

salt and freshly ground black pepper

1½ tablespoons chopped fresh thyme, or 1½ teaspoons dried and crumbled

1 cup flour

one (3½- to 4-pound) roasting chicken, cut into 8 pieces

1 tablespoon canola oil

3 cups dry red wine

1 bay leaf

½ cup finely chopped fresh parsley

11 ounces crimini mushrooms, or button mushrooms, washed gently and cut in half

In a large, heavy skillet, pot, or casserole, cook the bacon strips over moderate heat and let them crisp up; drain the cooked bacon on paper towels. Remove all but 1 tablespoon of the bacon grease in the skillet. Add ½ tablespoon of the olive oil to the bacon grease and place over low heat. Add the leek, scallions, pearl onions, carrots, salt, pepper, and thyme and cook, stirring occasionally, for 10 minutes.

Meanwhile, place the flour on a large plate and season liberally with salt and pepper. Dry off the chicken pieces with a paper towel and then dredge them in the seasoned flour, making sure all sides are well coated.

In a large, heavy skillet, heat 1 tablespoon canola oil and ½ tablespoon of the olive oil over high heat. Brown the chicken, a few pieces at a time, about 3 minutes per side, being careful not to crowd the skillet, adding the additional oil if needed. If the chicken or the oil starts to burn, reduce the heat to moderate. Remove the browned pieces of chicken to paper towels or a brown paper grocery bag to drain off any excess fat.

Preheat the oven to 325 degrees.

When the vegetables are tender, sprinkle in 2 tablespoons flour from the flour you used to dredge the chicken. Let cook 2 minutes, stirring occasionally. Raise the heat to high and add the wine and the bay leaf, letting it come to a rolling boil. Add the chicken pieces, spooning the wine over the chicken so it is almost completely bathed in it. Sprinkle on half the parsley. Cover the casserole and place on the middle shelf of the preheated oven. Bake for 1 hour, basting the chicken pieces once or twice during that time.

After an hour, add the mushrooms, baste the chicken, make sure the mushrooms are coated in the wine sauce, cover, and bake another 30 minutes. Remove from the oven.

Serve hot, sprinkled with the remaining parsley.

### Tips

*You want a really well-rounded red wine, not too fruity. Choose something you would like to drink with dinner or a lesser wine made from the same grape as what you'll serve with the stew.*

*Don't place the mushrooms under cold running water to clean. Use a vegetable brush and lightly scrub the mushroom caps clean using just a tiny bit of water. Excess water will be absorbed by the mushroom, creating a watery dish.*

# Maine Shrimp, Haddock, and Jerusalem Artichoke Winter Chowder

Jerusalem artichokes give this Maine shrimp-based chowder a great crunchy texture and sweet flavor. The chowder can be made a few hours (or a day) ahead of time and simply reheated over low heat until bubbling hot. This chowder is a great platform for showing off the shrimp's sweet, fresh winter flavor.

*Serves 4*

> 3 strips bacon, optional
> 1 tablespoon olive oil
> 1 medium onion, finely chopped
> salt and freshly ground black pepper
> 1 tablespoon chopped fresh thyme, or 1 teaspoon dried and crumbled
> 1 pound potatoes, peeled and chopped into 1/2-inch cubes,
>      Yukon Gold works well
> 1/2 pound Jerusalem artichokes, peeled and chopped into 1/2-inch pieces
> 1 1/2 cups low-fat milk
> 1 cup cream
> 1 pound haddock, cut into 1-inch cubes
> 1 to 1 1/2 tablespoons flour
> 1/3 cup finely chopped fresh parsley
> 1 pinch cayenne pepper
> 1 pound peeled whole Maine shrimp

In a large soup pot, cook the bacon until crisp on both sides; drain on paper towels. Crumble the bacon into small pieces and set aside. Remove all but 1 tablespoon of the bacon grease.

Add the oil to the bacon grease (if you choose not to add bacon, work with about 1 1/2 tablespoons olive oil instead). Add the onion to the hot oil and cook, stirring frequently, over low heat for about 8 minutes, or until the onions are soft and just beginning to turn color. Add the salt, pepper, and half the thyme, and stir well. Add the potatoes and artichokes and cook, stirring, for a minute to coat the potatoes and artichokes thoroughly with the spices and onions.

Meanwhile heat the milk and cream in a small saucepan over moderate heat until just simmering.

Add the haddock to the pot with the onions and potatoes and stir well. Sprinkle on the flour and stir gently to coat all the ingredients. Let cook about 2 minutes. Add half the crumbled bacon (if using), the remaining thyme, and then the warm milk and cream. Raise the heat and bring to a gentle simmer. Once the chowder simmers, reduce the heat to low, add half the parsley and the cayenne. Cover and let cook for 10 to 15 minutes, or until the potatoes are tender. Add the shrimp and cook for 4 to 5 minutes, or until they firm up. Taste for seasoning, and add more salt, pepper, and cayenne if needed.

Serve hot with a sprinkling of parsley and some of the remaining bacon on top.

### Tips

*You need one tablespoon of flour as a thickener, but if you prefer a thinner chowder, only add this amount. If you want a thicker, more stew-like soup, add 1½ tablespoons flour.*

*You'll need 2½ cups dairy — for a lighter chowder add all milk and for a richer one add the cream. You can play with the proportions of milk and cream depending on how rich you like it.*

---

### ⇒❋ Maine Shrimp: How Sweet They Are ❋⇐

*Everyone knows about Maine lobster. But what about Maine shrimp? Shrimp are one of the state's best-kept culinary secrets. Maine shrimp are pink, quite small (only about three to four inches long unpeeled), and exceedingly sweet. Unlike their farm-raised cousins, who come to American fish markets rock-hard frozen from Southeast Asia and Latin America, they don't command a very high price. Some cooks and connoisseurs say Pandalus borealis, or Maine shrimp, have a sweet flavor closer to Maine lobster than the imported shrimp most of us are familiar with.*

*Maine's shrimp season is short — from January until the end of February or March — generally around six weeks, though in a good year you'll find the season extended until the beginning of May. Maine shrimp are well worth finding, and freeze well. If you can find peeled Maine shrimp it's worth paying the extra few dollars because peeling these tiny things, with their sharp shells, is a real pain.*

*Maine shrimp need to cook for only about a minute or two, so you don't want to use them with heavy sauces or elaborate cooking techniques. Quick stir-fries, sautés, or a simple sauce for pasta, or rice dishes, or added to soups at the last minute is your best bet.*

# February

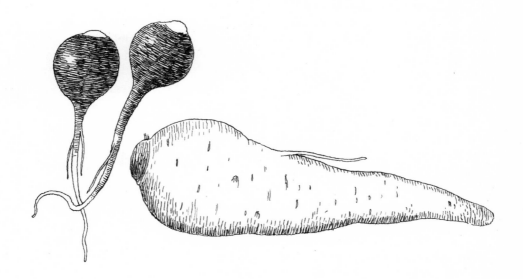

# THE RISE OF
# WINTER FARMERS' MARKETS

Eat local. Shop local. These mantras of the local and Slow Food movements are words to live by — unless, of course, you happen to spend your winters in northern New England. How is anyone supposed to eat local in the dead of winter when the land is covered in ice and snow and nothing is growing?

Yes, I get fresh eggs from our small flock of chickens, and there is a dairy nearby that makes wonderful yogurt and cheese. But putting together meals based on local food all year long in Maine takes careful planning. And even then the strategy doesn't always work.

In the fall I fill my freezer with locally raised meat and poultry, beans and other vegetables from my garden, and local fruit. I just enjoyed the last of my raspberries in a pie served on a day when the temperature plunged to 12 degrees. I still have a few jars of the peaches I picked last September, steeped in brandy and waiting to be poured over ice cream or a lemon cake. These foods are highlights of my winter cooking, but there's never enough to last the whole season.

To fill in the considerable gaps, I shop carefully at local markets, but it's nearly impossible to avoid buying vegetables grown in California, Florida, or places even more distant. Plus, I really like bananas and avocados all year long.

Recently I've noticed that eating local in the winter is getting a little easier. Throughout Maine and, just across the border in New Hampshire, winter farmers' markets have cropped up. At last count Maine offered over a dozen winter farmers' markets from Bath to Camden, Portland to Skowhegan. They are starting to change the way Mainers shop and eat in the winter and, perhaps even more importantly, changing the economic realities for many Maine farmers.

It's 24 degrees, a bright, sunny February morning. I grab my nylon and canvas shopping bags (I feel so virtuous when I actually remember to bring my reusable bags shopping) and head off to the Seacoast Winter Farmer's Market, just over the border in Rollinsford, New Hampshire. Twice a month from November through April, York County farmers and their counterparts in Rockingham and Strafford counties, New Hampshire, assemble in greenhouses and town halls throughout the Seacoast to sell everything from locally raised eggs and meat to winter greens, root vegetables, cheese, fish, and hot-house tomatoes.

The market officially opens at ten, but people begin pouring in just before nine. The response to the market can be summed up with three numbers: 2, 2,200, and 45. Two is the number of policemen employed to manage the traffic flow outside the market; 2,200 is the estimated number of shoppers who came on a cold winter morning to buy local produce. That puts a huge smile on the faces of the forty five farmers, bakers, and vendors selling their products inside.

Garen Heller, a farmer who runs Garen's Greens at Riverside Farm in North Berwick, Maine, describes the turnout in one word: "unreal! It's just unbelievable what is happening here. These crowds mean a return to the roots of people valuing agriculture. It's a cult of agriculture." When I ask Heller what the winter farmer's market means for his business, he doesn't hesitate. "I can breathe a little easier without worrying about income. These markets didn't exist three years ago. If things continue on this trajectory, it's going to change what it means to be a farmer in northern New England."

About an hour after the market opens, Heller is already sold out of his greenhouse-grown salad greens, winter radishes, bok choy, kale, and mustard greens. Early shoppers know to head straight for his table and grab the coveted produce.

As I walk the aisles of the market, held in a modern greenhouse flooded with winter sun, I see people lining up to buy root vegetables (everything from celery root, purple-topped turnips, and carrots to potatoes and parsnips), greens (chard, kale, and mixed salad greens), locally raised meats (chicken, pork, and beef, as well as buffalo and elk), locally caught fish (lobster, Maine winter shrimp, sole, haddock, and fresh crabmeat), locally made yogurt and milk, maple syrup, honey, cheese, bread, and pastries. If you get to market early enough, you can buy virtually everything a family needs for a week's-worth of good eating.

Prices are definitely higher here than at the grocery store. "In a down economy like this its even more exciting that people are willing to spend more and see the value of local food," says Heller. "I would love to see local foods become more available to all people. There is a certain elitism to this market, but I gotta tell you, I've seen a lot of different types of people here today from all over."

People eat hot soup and homemade chili, sip on hot, spiced local cider. A group of folk musicians pick at banjoes and guitars at one end of the greenhouse, while shoppers, dressed in down jackets and thick, furry boots, greet one another over bins of onions and samples of granola. I stand in a corner, pen and pad in hand, and just listen to the snippets of conversation around me.

"It makes you feel good about living in Maine again, doesn't it?"

"Michael Pollan would approve of this market so much!"

"I haven't eaten anything really fresh in months. This is so exciting!"

"Oh-my-God, look, something green!"

"I just want to hug all these farmers and thank them for growing such gorgeous food so we can eat well all winter!"

It hits me. This is my community, my neighbors coming out to support farmers and let them know how much they matter to us all on a cold, sunny Saturday morning in February. It's like bearing witness to something new, something important to northern New England. We don't have to eat food we don't want to eat. We have choices.

Over by the coffee and baked goods, I spot John Forti, a garden historian, and Curator of Historic Gardens and Landscapes at Strawbery Banke Museum in nearby Portsmouth, New Hampshire, and co-founder of Slow Food Seacoast. He is smiling and waving to every third or fourth person who walks by. "This market," says Forti, "is just the best winter social event around."

Even after their bags are filled, people linger and catch up with friends and neighbors. When is the last time you saw someone happily hanging out in a grocery store?

Forti is known in the community as a big supporter of anything to do with local food. "Greg Brown sings a song called "The Poet Game," and in it he says, 'I watched my country turn into a coast-to-coast strip mall and I cried out in a song: if we could do all that in thirty years, then please tell me you all — why does good change take so long?' This market makes me think of bringing good change."

All the people involved with winter farmers' markets that I spoke with have the same message. In order to make this work on a larger scale, we need to involve local grocery stores and smaller shops year-round. I know that when I walk into my grocery store in June, at the peak of the local strawberry season, and see firm, juiceless, pink berries that have been trucked in from California, it makes me angry. I make sure to see a manager and ask him/her why they aren't selling local fruit when it's in season? You might try doing the same thing. Many big chain supermarkets in New England, and across the country, are calling attention to farm-raised food with signs that point out "Locally Grown." Grocery stores face lots of competition. Let them know that you *want* them to carry foods that are local and regional. Speak up and tell them it's important to you. During the winter months there is no reason why big supermarkets can't offer carrots, parsnips, onions, potatoes, and winter squash from local farmers.

You know the bumper stick: "No Farms, No Food." If we want to eat well, and keep the local food movement alive and well, it's a slogan we'll need to seriously consider.

# Winter Salad *of* Balsamic–Glazed Turnips *and* Baby Greens

I grew up believing that turnips were big, white waxed vegetables with a starchy, awful taste. Then I tasted small, baseball-size, purple-topped turnips, roasted them in a 400 degree oven, and was wowed! Turnips are sweet and juicy and make for excellent winter eating. Here they are roasted and tossed with balsamic vinegar (which gives them a gorgeous glaze) and served with mixed winter greens.

*Serves 4*

### For the turnips:

1 pound small or medium purple-topped or white turnips, greens ends trimmed
1½ tablespoons olive oil
salt and freshly ground black pepper
1½ tablespoons balsamic vinegar

### For the salad and vinaigrette:

1½ teaspoons Dijon-style mustard
salt and freshly ground black pepper
1 tablespoon plain yogurt
1 tablespoon red or white wine vinegar
½ tablespoon balsamic vinegar
3 tablespoons olive oil
4 cups baby mixed greens, (baby arugula, spinach, sprouts)

Preheat the oven to 400 degrees. Cut large turnips into quarters, medium-size ones in half, and leave small (1-inch or so) turnips whole. Place in a medium-size roasting pan or oven-proof skillet and toss with the olive oil, salt, and pepper. Roast for 15 minutes. Add the balsamic and toss to coat all the turnips. Roast another 15 or 20 minutes, tossing the turnips once or twice so they brown evenly on both sides, and roast until they are just tender when pierced with a small sharp knife. Remove from the oven and let cool 5 to 10 minutes, until they are warm.

In a small bowl, mix the mustard, salt, and pepper. Stir in the yogurt. Add the vinegars and then the oil and stir to make a smooth dressing. The vinaigrette can be made several hours ahead of time. Cover and refrigerate until ready to use.

Meanwhile, place the greens in the center of a large plate or bowl. Arrange the warm turnips around the edges of the salad plate or bowl. Serve the dressing on the side.

# Maine Crab Cakes

A crab cake should taste like sweet fresh crabmeat — not red pepper or spices or celery or anything else. Maine crabmeat never really gets it due; it always seems to be ignored in favor of its famed cousin, the lobster. But Maine's crabmeat is exceptionally sweet and meaty and reasonably priced.

With these simple crab cakes, I sauté a very small bit of onion and scallions until they are soft and sweet and then season the mixture with fresh ginger (which, rather than detracting from the flavor of the crab, seems to heighten it). Double the recipe and have a party. I serve these cakes with lemon wedges, hot sauce, or Better Than Tartar Sauce *(page 19)*.

*Serves 4*

    1 tablespoon olive oil
    1 small onion, finely chopped
    1 scallion, finely chopped
    1 tablespoon finely chopped fresh ginger
    1 tablespoon minced fresh chives, optional
    salt and freshly ground black pepper
    8 ounces fresh Maine crabmeat
    1 egg, lightly whisked
    1 teaspoon lemon zest
    1 cup Panko breadcrumbs, plus 1/3 cup
    about 1 1/2 tablespoons canola oil

In a medium skillet, heat the olive oil over low heat. Add the onion and cook for 4 minutes, stirring occasionally. Add the scallion, ginger, half the chives, if using, a touch of salt and pepper, and cook, stirring, another minute. Remove from the heat.

Place the crab in a medium bowl. Add the remaining chives, if using. Add the egg, lemon zest, sautéed onion mixture, a touch of salt and pepper, and 1/3 cup of the breadcrumbs, and mix gently until everything is well incorporated. To test the mixture, gather about 1/2 cup and form into a small cake; it should hold together without crumbling or falling apart. If it falls apart, add an additional tablespoon or so of breadcrumbs. Form the mixture into eight 2-inch cakes.

Place the remaining cup of breadcrumbs on a plate or bowl and *very lightly* coat the outsides of the crab cake with the breadcrumbs — you only want a very light coating. If making the crab cakes ahead of time, place on a small baking sheet, cover, and chill until ready to cook.

Heat the canola oil in a large skillet over moderately high heat. When the oil is hot (drop a speck of breadcrumb in the oil; it should sizzle), add a few crab cakes at a time, being careful not to crowd the pan, and cook for 3 to 4 minutes on each side, or until golden brown and hot. Drain on paper towel and serve hot with lemon wedges, hot sauce, or Better Than Tartar Sauce.

---

# Lamb Burgers *with* Chopped Walnuts, Mint, *and* Yogurt

Look for local lamb or ask the butcher to ground good quality natural lamb for you. The crunch of finely chopped walnuts mixed with the ground meat, yogurt, and chopped fresh mint and cilantro makes an amazingly moist and well-flavored burger. Grill them outside if you can (so what if it's 5 degrees out?), or you can pan-fry them in a skillet with a touch of olive oil.

*Serves 4*

> 1 pound ground lamb
> 1 scallion, very thinly chopped
> 2 tablespoons yogurt
> 3 tablespoons finely chopped walnuts
> 2 tablespoons chopped fresh mint
> 2 tablespoons chopped fresh cilantro
> salt and freshly ground black pepper
> accompaniments: plain yogurt, ketchup, pita bread heated on the grill
>     or in a warm oven

In a large bowl, mix the lamb, scallion, yogurt, walnuts, mint, cilantro, salt, and pepper until fully combined. Divide the mixture into four patties. The burgers can be made several hours ahead of time. Cover and refrigerate.

Put on your gloves and coat and go out there and heat a grill — charcoal, wood, or gas — until medium-hot. Place the burgers over the direct heat and cook about 4 to 5 minutes on each side, (you can do this in a skillet inside, too), or until the lamb is cooked through and only slightly pink. Serve hot with warm pita bread, yogurt, and ketchup, if desired.

# Roasted Root Vegetable Salad *with* Basil Vinaigrette *and* Crumbled Feta

When the variety of fresh produce gets you down (meaning the only thing fresh you can find at the farmer's market or stores are roots, roots, and more root vegetables), you have to get creative. This salad combines three popular New England root vegetables, but you could easily add or substitute others. Thin slices of parsnips, carrots, and onions are roasted until caramelized and tender, and then lightly sprinkled with a fresh basil vinaigrette and crumbled feta cheese. It's a salad that so transcends the genre that your taste buds will forget it's still mid-winter.

Use beets, potatoes, garlic, turnip, celery root, and leeks as well. You can easily double or triple the quantities to serve a larger number. The only trick is to make sure that all the vegetables are cut into similarly sized pieces so they will roast evenly. The vegetables can be roasted a day ahead of time (cover and refrigerate until ready to assemble the salad). Serve with crusty bread.

*Serves 4*

1/2 pound carrots, peeled and cut into 1/4-inch slices
1/2 pound parsnips, peeled and cut into 1/4-inch slices
1 medium onion, about 1/2 pound, peeled and cut into 1/4-inch slices
1/4 cup olive oil
sea salt and freshly ground black pepper
1/4 cup thinly sliced fresh basil, or coarsely chopped fresh parsley
11/2 tablespoons red or white wine vinegar
1/3 cup crumbled feta cheese

Preheat the oven to 425 degrees.

On a large baking tray or rimmed cookie sheet, toss the carrots, parsnips, and onion with about 2 tablespoons of the oil. Add the salt and pepper. Arrange the vegetables in a single layer and place on the middle shelf. Roast for 15 minutes. Toss the vegetables and rearrange in a single layer. Roast for another 10 minutes, or until the vegetables have begun to brown and they feel tender when tested with a small sharp knife. Remove from the oven and let cool.

Arrange the roasted vegetables on a medium platter or oval plate. Scatter the basil on top and drizzle with the vinegar and remaining oil. Season with salt and pepper. Scatter the cheese along the edges of the plate and sprinkle some in the middle.

# DARK, COLD, AND SWEET:
# CHOCOLATE IN FEBRUARY

Yes, the days are definitely getting a bit longer, but they are also a whole lot colder. Nighttime hits hard. We've been doing a lot of staying home, and cooking. No complaints from me. But I have been having trouble almost every night around 7 P.M., when I get this overwhelming craving, like a force sweeping over me, to eat something sweet. Well, not just anything sweet. Chocolate. It must be chocolate.

I try to ignore it. I really do. I focus on work or watch a good movie, but like most addictions it invades my psyche. Most nights I simply give in by eating a few chocolate chips or a square of dark or bittersweet chocolate. I have finally become a chocolate grown-up and given up my lust for milk chocolate. It took years, and trying all kinds of chocolate to realize that to truly *taste* the quality of cacao you must eat it without the addition of dairy. Bittersweet, semi-sweet, or dark is the way to go!

Sometimes my chocolate cravings are even more specific: Once I wanted, no, I *needed*, dark chocolate, preferably highlighted with some really good sea salt. (Chocolate and sea salt are *very* good friends. They bring out the best in each other. If you don't believe me, just try the two together.) Rather than fight, I gave in, and set out to bake a chocolate tart sprinkled with Maine sea salt.

Late-night cravings and last-minute guests are two of the best reasons for having a well-stocked pantry. I found a bag of amaretti cookies (you know, those Italian almond cookies individually wrapped in tissue paper) that someone brought us over the holidays and we never got around to eating. I decided those crunchy sweet cookies would make an exceptional crust. I rummaged farther through the pantry and discovered a bar of 60 percent cocoa chocolate from Byrne & Carlson, one of my favorite local chocolate makers. (I suspect my husband, John, somewhat alarmed at this February chocolate frenzy of mine, hid the coveted bar in the far reaches of the pantry.) And then I discovered a jar of Maine sea salt, with its wonderful, coarse texture and briny full flavor.

A few hours later I cut thin slivers of the tart and sat down in front of the fire. "Where did you get this chocolate?" John asked innocently. "Shut up and taste it," I told him, cutting him a slice just slightly larger than mine. He didn't say another word — until he got around to asking for seconds.

# Rich Dark-Chocolate Tart *with* Maine Sea Salt

For this tart you make a simple crust by crushing amaretti cookies (or gingersnaps or chocolate or vanilla wafers) and mixing them with a touch of sugar and melted butter and lining a French tart pan. The filling is like a thick chocolate mousse — good bittersweet chocolate, cream, eggs, vanilla, and sea salt. What I love about the tart is that the filing has no sugar. It's all about honoring the chocolate and the balance of the sea salt.

Serve the tart in thin slices with hot chocolate (sure, why not, it's still February), dark coffee, or top it with vanilla-scented whipped cream, frozen yogurt, or crème fraîche.

The tart makes a wonderful Valentine's Day gift for someone you love. Even if they are the type who would hide chocolate from you. Plan on letting the tart cool for at least one hour and up to 12 hours. You'll need a 9-inch French-style round tart pan with a removable bottom for this tart; you can use a regular pie plate, but it's never quite as special.

*Serves 6 (or serves 2 for breakfast, lunch, and dinner)*

## For the crust:

1 cup ground amaretti cookies
5 tablespoons butter, melted
2 tablespoons sugar

## For the chocolate and sea salt filling:

1½ cups heavy cream
9 ounces bittersweet chocolate (65 percent cacao), well chopped,
    or 1½ cups semi-sweet chocolate chips
2 eggs
1 teaspoon vanilla extract
½ teaspoon good sea salt, plus some for sprinkling on top
2 tablespoons toasted coconut flakes, optional

Preheat the oven to 350 degrees.

In a bowl, mix the crushed cookies, the melted butter, and the sugar. Press the crust into a 9-inch round fluted tart pan. Press the crust into the bottom and up the sides of the pan.

Place the tart pan on a cookie sheet and bake on the middle shelf for 10 minutes. Remove and let cool for 10 minutes.

For the filling, place the cream in a medium saucepan and bring to a gentle simmer.

Place the chocolate in a large mixing bowl. Pour the hot cream on top and stir steadily, until the chocolate is completely melted and the mixture is smooth.

In a separate bowl, whisk the eggs, vanilla, and 1/2 teaspoon of the sea salt until frothy. Add the whisked egg mixture to the chocolate mixture. Pour the filling into the cooled crust and bake on the middle shelf for 25 to 28 minutes. To test for doneness, shake the tart gently, and if the middle wobbles a little (and still appears undercooked) but the sides seem solid, it is perfect. The tart will continue to cook when it's removed from the oven and will firm up while cooling.

Remove from the oven and, while the tart is still warm, sprinkle with an additional 1/2 teaspoon of the salt, and the coconut flakes, if using. *Very gently* press into the chocolate if it doesn't seem to adhere. Let the tart cool for 1 hour. Some claim the tart is best served after an hour of cooling, but I like it best after it's been covered and placed in the refrigerator for several hours, or overnight.

### Tips

*You'll need about 20 to 30 cookies, depending on the brand and the size. Place the cookies in a food processor or blender and blend until finely ground. You can also place them in a tightly sealed plastic bag and crush them with a rolling pin until finely ground. You could also substitute with ginger snaps, graham crackers, vanilla wafers, or chocolate graham crackers; 20 gingersnaps equals 1 1/2 cups ground cookies. And you can use 1 to 2 tablespoons toasted coconut flakes (unsweetened) instead of, or in addition to, the sugar in the crust.*

*Toasted coconut flakes are found in specialty food shops. But you can easily make them: place unsweetened coconut flakes on a cookie sheet and bake at 350 degrees until the flakes just begin to turn a golden brown, about 10 minutes. Remove and cool.*

# Triple Chocolate *and* Macadamia Nut Biscotti

These biscotti, twice-baked Italian cookies, are flavored with orange juice, orange zest, macadamia nuts, and chocolate.

Chocolate appears three times in the recipe: cocoa powder is sifted into the flour mixture, chocolate is added to the biscotti mixture, and then, after the cookies have been baked twice, they are dipped in melted bittersweet chocolate. They are the kind of treat that isn't all that bad for you because they use very little butter, no cream, or other fats. And because they are baked twice they have a fabulous crisp, crunchy texture.

Biscotti are excellent for dipping into cappuccino, coffee, tea, or hot cocoa. They will keep for about a week if you store them in a tightly sealed tin or plastic bag and keep in a dark, cool spot.

*Makes 28 to 30 biscotti*

> 2 cups raw macadamia nuts, or any other nut you prefer
> 2 cups plus 2 tablespoons flour, plus more for dusting
> 1 cup sugar
> 1/3 cup unsweetened cocoa powder
> 1 1/2 teaspoons baking powder
> 1/2 teaspoon salt
> 4 tablespoons unsalted butter (1/2 stick), cold, cut into 4 pieces
> 2 large eggs
> 1 teaspoon vanilla
> 1 1/2 packed teaspoons grated orange or tangerine zest
> 1/4 cup orange or tangerine juice, preferably fresh
> 1 1/2 cups good quality semi-sweet or bittersweet chocolate chips, about 55 percent cacao, or 8 ounces semi-sweet or bittersweet chocolate, well chopped

Place a rack in the center of the oven and preheat the oven to 350 degrees. Line a cookie sheet with parchment paper or a silicon mat.

Coarsely chop the macadamia nuts and place on another cookie sheet. Bake on the middle shelf for 8 to 10 minutes, or until you can smell the nuts and they begin to turn a very pale golden brown; set aside.

In a large bowl, sift the flour, sugar, cocoa powder, baking powder, and salt. Add the butter and blend into the dry ingredients using your fingertips or a pastry cutter, until the mixture resembles coarse sand. In another small bowl, whisk the eggs, vanilla, zest, and juice until well blended. Add the wet ingredients to the dry ingredients and stir with a wooden spoon until just blended. Fold in the nuts and 1/2 cup of the chocolate.

Generously flour a clean working area. Using floured hands, divide the dough into two equal portions. Form each piece of dough into a flat log roughly 12 inches long by 2 inches wide by 1 inch high, adding additional flour as needed to prevent the dough from sticking to the work surface. Carefully place the logs 2 to 3 inches apart on the parchment-covered baking sheet.

Bake the logs for 30 minutes, or until firm to the touch. Remove from the oven, reduce the oven temperature to 300 degrees, and let the biscotti cool for 15 minutes.

Transfer the logs to a cutting board. Using a sharp, serrated knife and a gentle sawing motion, cut logs on a slight diagonal into 1/2-inch-wide pieces. Place the biscotti cut side up on 1 or 2 cookie sheets. Bake for 15 minutes. Remove and gently flip the biscotti over to the opposite side and bake for another 15 to 20 minutes. The biscotti should be firm to the touch. Remove from the baking sheet and cool completely on wire racks.

While the biscotti are cooling, melt the remaining chocolate in a small saucepan over *very* low heat. When almost all of the chocolate has melted, remove from the heat and let rest for 5 minutes. Dip half of each biscotti into the still-warm chocolate and hold vertically to let excess chocolate drip off. Place the biscotti on wax paper to cool until the chocolate hardens, 3 to 4 hours. The biscotti will keep, in a cool, dark, well-sealed tin or plastic bag, for several days.

# March

# SWEET TIMES, MAPLE SEASON

I get grumpy in March. All over the country people are celebrating the beginning of spring. My friend from northern California calls with reports of "gorgeous, aromatic" flowering trees and fields of yellow and white jonquils. She describes the weather as "perfect." I threaten to hang up on her. Even in New York City the bulbs are inches high, peeking their heads out of the urban earth and announcing the end of winter. But here in Maine the piles of white, now turning a distinctly unattractive shade of gray, are ever present. Old snow sits in huge discarded heaps in the driveway, in the fields across the street, and in parking lots all over town. It is a constant reminder that spring in Maine has not arrived, and won't come until it damn well feels like it.

There is an upside to March and it sounds like this: *drip, drip, drip.* At a time of year when nature offers so little hope, maple trees produce a clear, unassuming-looking liquid, which tastes like barely sweetened water. But weeks later, after much boiling and sweet steam evaporation, a golden amber syrup appears. Maple syrup season is, without a doubt, the best part of March in Maine.

My husband, John, and I are what you might call small-time home syrup makers. We only tap a half dozen or so maple trees scattered around our property. The ritual of cleaning out the taps, the old tin buckets, and thin lids (which we have gathered over the years at yard sales, farm foreclosures, and country stores) is actually something I look forward to. During this time of year the closest I actually get to growing food is to fantasize about it while I gaze at seed catalogs piled up on my desk, luring me with sexy pictures of tomatoes and basil and squash popping out of warm fertile earth. So getting outside and starting to "make" food thrills me.

Maple season means working with the weather (you need warm days and below-freezing nights for maximum sap flow) to make something delicious and truly of Maine. When the sap really starts flowing we spend hours outside straining it into buckets and getting ready to start the long, slow boiling process.

It's 10 P.M. and John is missing. I'm in bed, feeling my eyes droop, exhausted from this not-quite-winter-and-not-quite-spring limbo we're in. I call out to say goodnight and there's no answer. Then I hear him outside clanging around in the dark. This is not a man prone to disappearing or making strange noises in the dead of night, but it's maple season and he takes the dog and the newspaper out to the barn where he spends hours pouring the day's sap into huge metal pans. We used to cook the sap inside on the woodstove, but the sweet condensation started building up on the beams above the stove and we thought we saw ants appearing and suddenly there was nothing romantic or smart about boiling syrup indoors. John rigged up a strange outdoor maple cooker system. He sets the low metal trays (like high-sided lasagna pans) on top of a large, gas-fueled camping cooker and sits there watching the sap evaporate *slowly*.

When I use the word "slowly" I'm talking about Zen *slowly*, the kind of slowly where you sit for hours (and hours and hours) watching sap go from watery thin to kindasorta thin. Hours go by and nothing appears to be happening. Well, nothing that the untrained eye can see. It takes forty gallons of sap to make just one gallon of syrup. *It's all about process.* It takes almost a week of diligent boiling, adding bucketfuls of new sap each day, for this subtly sweet, water-like substance to resemble anything even remotely syrup-like. Once the sap hits the final stage (meaning the texture is thick enough to coat a spoon) it needs to be filtered through cheesecloth to remove any particles that might cloud the finished syrup.

The first few days of maple season I feel compelled to throw on my down jacket and head out into the cold, dark night to keep John company. He's generally pretty friendly and polite, but after a while I can tell that this barn/boiling time is a solitary kind of thing. A man, his dog, and his sap. I think the entire experience — the tapping of the trees, the putting up of the buckets, the collecting of the sap, the boiling, is all a meditative exercise for him. And I say: Go for it. Make me some gorgeous syrup and I'll cook you some gorgeous food.

He comes inside the house and climbs into bed at all hours of the night, mumbling sweet nothings into my ear. "We're almost there! Looking good! Almost syrup time." I roll over, fantasizing about all the wonderful things I'll cook when the syrup is finally done.

And then, after nights of climbing into bed alone, I'll wake up one fine March morning and see that first jar of syrup, the color of topaz. Pale topaz. He always leaves a few tablespoons in a bowl on the table for me to taste. Every year I swear it's the best syrup we've ever made. About that point of ownership: I like to think of it as *our* syrup, from *our* maple trees, made at *our* house, but there's no doubt in John's mind that it's *his* syrup. In all fairness, I guess since he's the one who stays up late on all those cold March nights, he should be awarded the title of Master Syrup Maker.

We've learned a lot over the years. Turns out that maple syrup, like wine, has good years and bad ones — years when the sap flows like water from the tap and others when it's just too rainy and the sap gets diluted with rainwater. And there are days when it turns warm too early and the sap clouds over and gives off a slightly sour smell. Every few years John insists on giving the trees a year off, like they're athletes in danger of being over-trained. He claims he doesn't want to overtax them, but it's hard to give up a year of maple syrup. I guess I'm just not Zen enough to let it go.

The first batch of syrup, what we call "First Run" (and what would be called Grade A or Light Amber if it were sold commercially) is a pale golden color. The flavor is light and subtle, with a pure maple essence. It's the texture that's really extraordinary. A thinish syrup that coats your tongue with its subtle sweetness and smooth, buttery feel.

The notion of *terroir*, coming from the French word *terre*, meaning "land" or "earth," refers to the impact a specific piece of land lends to food that's grown or made on it. It's a term wine makers like to throw around, but it also applies to the making of cheese (think Roquefort or Parmesan) and coffee (Kona or Blue Mountain) or even beef (Kobe). But I think it's also an appropriate term to consider in the making of maple syrup. If my land and trees and old farmhouse could be distilled into a single taste, I think this First Run maple syrup would express it well. Clean, sweet, complex, and deeply pleasing.

We try to save the precious, small First Run batch for really important meals, like pouring over the first blueberry pancakes of the year, or drizzling it over locally made yogurt. Sometimes I sip it by the teaspoonful directly from the jar and am simply wowed that anything can be so sweet, so buttery, and naturally rich. I have come to think of this First Run syrup as "liquid gold."

I've been experimenting with the second and third runs, the darker, stronger, more molasses-like syrup (labeled as Medium, Dark, and Extra Dark Amber) as much as possible, and not just in the standard breakfast kind of dishes. I glaze nuts — walnuts, almonds, pecans, and pistachios — in syrup and serve them in salads or as a snack. I like to spoon a few tablespoons of syrup on top of sautéed slices of thick country ham or chicken breasts, and salmon filets (it creates an almost instant caramelized glaze if you add it to a hot sauté pan), or drizzle it over thick slices of winter squash or sweet potatoes and roast them until they're soft and sweet and practically melt in your mouth. Extra-dark amber syrup makes extraordinary full-flavored maple ice cream.

One of my new favorites is maple-glazed bacon. Take a few strips of thick country bacon (from a good butcher and not those pitiful, water-injected, thin slices you find suffocating in plastic at the grocery store) and place them on a broiler tray or baking sheet. Brush the bacon liberally with maple syrup, sprinkle on some chili power, and place the tray under the broiler for a minute or two. Flip the bacon over, brush it again with syrup and chili powder, and broil it on the other side until it's cooked through, crisp, and caramelized. The combination of sweet syrup, fiery chilis, and fatty pork is unforgettable. Eat it for breakfast, crumbled on salads, or serve the bacon with cocktails, like grown-up candy.

When you're involved in making your own food (even if it's simply a matter of collecting sap from a tree and boiling it down), it becomes precious. I am aware of every tablespoon of syrup I use, thankful that I'm married to a man crazy enough to spend long, freezing hours in an icy, dust-filled barn watching thin water turn to magical amber-gold syrup. Mostly I'm just grateful for the miracle of the syrup itself, with all its natural sweetness, and the way it lets me know that the seasons are finally changing.

## ⇶ Maple Syrup Facts ⇷

◆ A gallon of pure maple syrup weighs around eleven pounds.

◆ One large maple tree can release as much as forty to sixty gallons of sap. That may sound like a huge amount of sap, but keep in mind that it takes forty gallons of sap to make one gallon of syrup.

◆ Maple trees are generally not tapped until they are at least twelve inches in diameter. Tapping younger trees can harm them.

◆ Maple syrup is three times sweeter than cane sugar, but contains only forty calories per tablespoon. A tablespoon of sugar contains forty-eight calories.

◆ The idea of tapping sap from sugar maple trees (Acer saccharum) was developed by Native Americans in the Northeast. They used syrup much like we use salt today — to season virtually everything. (Not a bad idea, really.) They traded syrup like money. The first syrup was made by dropping red-hot stones into thick wooden containers of sap, at a time before Europeans settlers arrived with fireproof vessels.

◆ Many small New England farmers still harvest sap the old-fashioned way by collecting the sap manually on a daily basis from buckets. But big-time producers now have intricate plastic tubing systems that carry the sap directly from the trees to the sugar house where it is boiled down.

◆ One of the great culinary March traditions in New England is maple on snow. Fresh snow is scooped up into a bowl and maple syrup is poured on top. The icy snow causes the syrup to harden a bit and make a kind of instant maple-flavored slurpy. Give it a try.

◆ Many cooks use maple syrup as a substitute for honey — in baking, savory recipes, even for sweetening coffee and tea.

45

# Maple Cheesecake *with* Maple-Ginger Crust

This is the time to use the darker, Grade B, fuller-flavored syrup. Maple syrup appears in this cake in three variations: it's in the crust along with ground gingersnaps; in the creamy filling mixed with cream cheese, eggs, and sour cream; and finally glazed onto the walnut halves that decorate the top of the cake. The cake can be made and baked a full day ahead of time. It will need at least six to eight hours to chill and set, so plan accordingly.

*Serves 8 to 10*

### For the crust:

2 cups ground gingersnaps (about 8 ounces)
1 stick unsalted butter, melted
3 tablespoons maple syrup

### For the filling:

four (8-ounce) packages of cream cheese, at room temperature
4 eggs
3/4 cup maple syrup
1 teaspoon vanilla extract
1/2 cup sour cream or crème fraîche

### For the maple-glazed walnuts:

1 1/2 tablespoons unsalted butter
1 teaspoon ground ginger
1/2 pound (8 ounces) walnut halves
3 tablespoons maple syrup

Preheat the oven to 350 degrees.

To make the crust: place the cookies in a food processor and process until finely ground. Place the ground cookies, melted butter, and syrup in a bowl and mix until well combined. Press the crust into the bottom and just up the sides of a 10-inch springform pan. Place a double layer of aluminum foil outside the pan, covering the bottom and sides of the pan to prevent any mixture from spilling out. Place in the refrigerator to chill for at least 10 minutes.

Meanwhile, make the filling. Place the cream cheese in the bowl of a standing mixer fitted with the paddle attachment. Beat the cream cheese on low, using a spatula frequently to make sure that the cream cheese is smooth and not clumping up along the sides of the bowl or on the paddle. This is a crucial step. Add the eggs, one at a time, beating well after each addition. Add the maple syrup, vanilla, and sour cream and beat until smooth, being careful not to overbeat it or let the mixture get too fluffy and airy.

Pour the filling into the chilled crust and place on a cookie sheet (to keep anything from spilling over). Bake on the middle shelf for about 1 hour and 5 minutes, or until the cheesecake is just beginning to take on a very pale maple color. When you jiggle the cake gently, the center will still appear to be wobbly — this is O.K. Remove the pan from the oven and let cool to room temperature.

While the cake is baking or cooling, prepare the walnuts: melt the butter in a large skillet over moderate heat. Add the ginger and cook for 10 seconds, stirring to incorporate the spice. Add the walnuts and cook, stirring for 2 minutes. Drizzle on the maple syrup, stir well to coat, and cook for another 2 minutes. Spread the nuts out on a sheet of parchment paper or aluminum foil, in a single layer, making sure they don't clump up.

When the cake is room temperature, carefully remove the sides of the pan, running a flat kitchen knife around the rim if it needs help separating. Decorate the top of the cake with the maple walnuts, creating a pattern along the edges and center of the cake. Very loosely cover the cake and chill for 6 hours or overnight. Do not place in refrigerator while the cake is still hot or warm.

# Whipped Maple Butter

I'm not sure why I didn't think of this sooner, but whipped fresh butter with maple syrup is like magic. The whipped sweet butter is amazing on morning toast, pancakes, French toast, waffles, muffins, scones, biscuits, or any morning treat. But it's equally good spread on a ham and cheese sandwich, or a sharp cheddar cheese and pear or apple sandwich. Try adding a tablespoon to sautéed chicken, salmon, or scallops and letting it melt and caramelize in the hot skillet or add a dash of cinnamon, cardamom, ground ginger, nutmeg, or allspice, or even a hit of chili powder.

*Makes ½ cup butter*

> **1 stick unsalted butter, at room temperature**
> **2½ tablespoons maple syrup**

In a standing mixer or using a hand-held mixer, whisk the butter for about 3 minutes, or until light and fluffy. Add the syrup and mix until well incorporated. It's best to use the butter soon or the syrup will begin to separate from the fats in the butter. Keep the butter covered and refrigerated for about a week. Stir or whip before serving if the butter appears separated.

# Grilled Salmon *with* Maple Glaze *and* Sea Salt

I am not a big fan of sweet sauces on fish. But the balance of rich oily salmon balanced by sweet maple syrup and coarse sea salt and freshly ground pepper works. The recipe is quite simple: Maple syrup is simmered down to a thick glaze and then brushed onto salmon fillets. Coarse sea salt and freshly ground pepper go on top, and the whole thing is placed under the broiler or on the grill. The salmon is basted twice with the reduced syrup. The result: moist salmon with a sweet and slightly salty glaze. Serve with basmati rice or cous cous, or for brunch with fried eggs and biscuits, muffins, or crusty bread.

*Serves 2*

> 6 tablespoons maple syrup
> 1 teaspoon olive oil
> two (6 to 8 ounce) salmon filets, or 1 pound salmon cut into two pieces
> 1/2 teaspoon sea salt
> coarsely ground black pepper

Place the syrup in a small saucepan and place over *very low heat*. Simmer for about 7 to 10 minutes, or until the syrup is thickened, and almost reduced by half.

Spread the oil along the bottom of a medium-size, rimmed baking sheet or gratin dish. Place the fish on top, skin side down. Using a pastry brush or the back of a spoon, lightly brush half the syrup on top of the fish. (If you reduced the syrup and it has "hardened," you'll need to reheat it over *very low* heat again to liquefy it and make it easy to work with.) Sprinkle the salt and a good grinding of pepper on top and gently press the salt crystals and pepper into the syrup so they stick.

Preheat the broiler. Alternately, you can heat a gas or charcoal grill and place a grill tray on it (a small perforated grill device that lets you grill something without having it stick). Let the grill get hot, about 400 degrees. Place the fish about four inches under the broiler or place on the hot grill. Cook for 5 minutes. Brush the remaining syrup on top and grill for another 4 to 5 minutes, or until just cooked through. Remove from the heat and serve hot.

# MAINE'S FIRST-OF-THE-SEASON DELICACY — PARSNIPS

I t's one of those raw March days where the air smells of spring, but the wind bites like winter. I call this a tease day. It's 60 degrees and sunny on Monday and then, come Tuesday, there's a wet, snowy blizzard. Welcome to spring in New England.

Despite the weather, I'm in my friend's garden harvesting vegetables. Yes, it's mid-March and you might think there's nothing growing, but you'd be wrong. Tiny green shoots sprout up through the spongy, over-saturated March earth. My shovel moves through the dirt easily and I push it down far, well beneath the green shoots. And there they are. I've been accused of being overly dramatic, but I'll tell you this: The sight of my shovel filled with fresh vegetables on a crappy March day is enough to bring tears to my eyes. Digging at this time of year is not a chore. It feels more like proof, evidence, that good days are to come. It's enough to make you believe in something. Whatever your something happens to be.

And there they are. Beige, carrot-shaped parsnips popping out of the ground covered in a nice coating of early spring dirt.

A parsnip may not be as sexy as a ripe tomato or fresh melon or perfumed basil, but it holds a whole lot of appeal in mid-March. I adore parsnips' subtly sweet, earthy flavor. They are so fresh I bite into one like it's a carrot. And while it's far better roasted or pureed or made into soup or cake, this parsnip qualifies as a first-of-the-season delicacy. Yup, I said delicacy.

You may wonder, as I did, why parsnips are harvested in the improbable month of March? I checked in with the farmer who plants a few acres of my friend's land down the street. "You plant parsnips in mid- to late summer and let them spend the winter underground," George Carpenter, of Old Fields Farm in South Berwick, Maine, told me. "They sit in hibernation mode, under the frozen, snowy, muddy, wet earth until March. As soon as the green shoots are visible above ground, it's time to pick them."

What happens is that parsnips stop growing over the winter, but the starches in this root vegetable turn to sugar. That means freshly dug March parsnips have an extraordinary sweetness (almost a rich flavor) that makes them worth seeking out.

Are parsnips always harvested in March? I asked Carpenter. Some farmers harvest in the fall, but Carpenter claims when he pulled some out in late September they were "only slightly better than store bought. Turns out where the soil is fluffy, they do well. Where it's more compact, they do less well, either misshapen or only small carrot size." In the spring, he advises, "It's vitally important to harvest as soon as the soil can be loosened, since once the tops form the root turns pithy and the tops will go to flower. So the harvest date is weather-dependent, and not calendar determined."

I head over to my friend's garden, shovel in hand, as soon as the report comes in that the green parsnip shoots are evident. About fifteen minutes later I head home with a basket of gorgeous, beige roots, some like delicate pencil-size carrots and others fat and almost juicy looking. I roast them with some carrots (and a drizzle of freshly harvested March maple syrup), steam some, and mash them into a sweet, pale puree that I pair with sautéed scallops, and then bake parsnip cupcakes, similar to a carrot cake. Gardening in March isn't nearly as crazy as it sounds.

---

### ⚔ Literary Roots ⚔

*It's rumored that Sarah Orne Jewett, the nineteenth-century writer who made her home in South Berwick, Maine, loved parsnip cake. On the anniversary of Jewett's birthday (she was born September 3, 1849), the folks at The Jewett House commissioned a local baker to prepare a parsnip cake. But when I asked Joanne Flaherty, the exhibitions coordinator for Historic New England, the organization that runs the Jewett House, why parsnip cake, she wrote back in an email: " ...We are unable to find why [parsnip] cakes have been used all these years or if there is any evidence of Jewett even liking parsnips..."*

*I then contacted Sarah Way Sherman, an English professor at the University of New Hampshire in Durham, a Jewett scholar, and author of the book* Sarah Orne Jewett, an American Persephone, *and she wasn't at all clear on the connection between Jewett and parsnips.*

*The only actual reference I could find comes from Jewett's story, "The Tory Lover," where she describes one of her characters as follows: "He was about beat, an' half froze anyway; his fingers looked like the p'ints o' parsnips. When he got back he laid right over acrost the cap. I left him up there a-clingin' on."*

# Roasted Parsnips *and* Carrots *with* Maple Glaze

Roasting root vegetables brings out their natural sweetness. You can also add onions, shallots, leeks, celery root (or celeriac), or turnips to this dish.

*Serves 4 to 6*

1 pound carrots, peeled, with root intact, washed
1 pound parsnips, peeled, with root intact, washed
1 tablespoon olive oil
salt and freshly ground black pepper
2 1/2 tablespoons maple syrup

Preheat the oven to 450 degrees.

Place the parsnips and carrots in a shallow, ovenproof gratin dish, skillet, or shallow casserole and toss with the oil, salt, and pepper. Place on the middle shelf of the oven and roast for 15 minutes. Toss and drizzle with the syrup. Roast for another 5 to 10 minutes, or until the vegetables are just tender when pierced with a small sharp knife. Remove and serve hot.

51

### Tip

*Look for tender, slender parsnips and carrots no thicker than an inch or so.*

## Sautéed Scallops *with* Parsnip Puree

The natural sweetness in parsnips pairs beautifully with sweet Maine scallops. A simple sauce is made by deglazing the sauté pan with garlic, white wine, and a touch of butter and chives.

*Serves 4*

### For the parsnip puree:

2 pounds young, thin parsnips, peeled, and cut into 1-inch pieces
1$^{1}/_{2}$ tablespoons crème fraîche, or sour cream
1 tablespoon butter
salt and freshly ground black pepper
1 teaspoon grated orange zest, optional

### For the scallops:

1 pound sea scallops
1 cup flour
salt and freshly ground black pepper
1 tablespoon olive oil
1 tablespoon butter
1 clove garlic, minced
1 cup dry white wine
1 tablespoon butter
2 tablespoon minced fresh chives

To make the puree, bring a medium pot of lightly salted water to a boil over high heat. Add the parsnips and cook over high heat for about 10 minutes, or until tender when pierced with a small sharp knife. Drain. Place the parsnips back in the pot and, using a potato masher, mash them until soft and somewhat smooth (parsnips won't get as smooth as potatoes do). Add the crème fraîche, butter, salt, pepper, and orange zest, if using, to taste. The puree can be made several hours ahead of time.

Use a paper towel to dry the scallops. Place the flour on a large plate and season, liberally, with the salt and pepper. Coat the scallops lightly on both sides.

Preheat the oven to 300 degrees.

In a large, heavy-bottomed skillet, heat the oil and butter over moderately-high heat. Add the garlic and cook, stirring, for 30 seconds; do not let it brown. Using a slotted spoon, remove the garlic from the oil and set off to the side. Add the scallops, being careful not to crowd the skillet and making sure they don't touch each other. Let cook for 2 minutes over high heat without touching them — they won't brown properly if you move them around or constantly check on them. Gently flip the scallops over and cook another 2 to 3 minutes, depending on the size. They should be a gorgeous golden-brown color. Remove to a serving plate and keep in the warm oven while you finish the sauce.

Add the wine to the hot skillet and let it simmer down over high heat for 5 to 6 minutes, or until thickened and reduced. Add the butter, salt, and a sprinkle of pepper and the reserved garlic, and cook for 1 minute. Sprinkle the chives into the sauce.

Place some parsnip puree in the center of a warm dinner plate, surround with the scallops, and spoon the sauce on top.

# Spiced Parsnip Cupcakes *with* Maple Cream Cheese Frosting, Toasted Walnuts, *and* Crystallized Ginger

I decided to transform traditional carrot cake into cupcakes, substituting fresh March parsnips, and topping them with a maple syrup–flavored cream cheese frosting, garnished with toasted walnuts and thin slivers of crystallized ginger. The cupcakes can be made and frosted several hours ahead of time; loosely cover and refrigerate until ready to serve. They are dedicated to Maine writer Sarah Orne Jewett *(page 50)*.

*Makes 12 cupcakes*

### For the parsnip cupcakes:

canola or vegetable oil spray for greasing the pans
1 cup walnuts
1¹/₂ cups flour
³/₄ cup sugar
2 tablespoons finely chopped crystallized ginger
2 teaspoons baking powder
1 teaspoon cinnamon
¹/₂ teaspoon ground ginger
¹/₂ teaspoon ground nutmeg
¹/₂ teaspoon salt
¹/₄ teaspoon allspice
3 large eggs
¹/₂ cup canola oil
¹/₂ cup buttermilk
about 5 parsnips or 3 medium–large carrots (11 ounces), peeled and
    shredded on the widest opening of a cheese grater

### For the maple cream cheese frosting and garnishes:

8 ounces cream cheese, at room temperature
6 tablespoons unsalted butter, at room temperature
³/₄ teaspoon vanilla extract
¹/₃ cup confectioners' sugar
2 to 3 tablespoons maple syrup
2 tablespoons crystallized ginger, cut into thin slivers

Spray 12 cupcake molds (1/2 cup size) with the vegetable oil spray, making sure the bottom and sides are well coated.

Preheat the oven to 350 degrees. Place the walnuts on a cookie sheet and bake on the middle shelf for about 8 minutes, or until fragrant. Remove and let cool. Finely chop half the walnuts and set aside; coarsely chop the remaining walnuts.

In a large bowl, mix the flour, sugar, crystallized ginger, and baking powder. Add the cinnamon, ground ginger, nutmeg, salt, and allspice, and mix well to combine all the spices with the flour and sugar.

In a separate bowl, whisk the eggs. Add the oil and buttermilk and whisk together. Add the egg/oil mixture to the flour/sugar mixture and mix. Add the shredded parsnips and the coarsely chopped walnuts, reserving the finely chopped walnuts for the final cupcake. Divide the batter between the 12 cupcake molds and bake on the middle shelf for 20 to 25 minutes, or until a toothpick inserted in the center comes out clean. Remove from the oven and let cool thoroughly.

Meanwhile, make the frosting. In a large bowl, mix the cream cheese and butter together until fully incorporated. They must be soft or you may need to use an electric mixer. Add the vanilla and mix thoroughly. Slowly add the sugar, bit by bit, making sure to incorporate it fully. Add the maple syrup and mix until smooth. The glaze will be thinner than a regular frosting; if it feels way too thin, you can refrigerate it for about 30 minutes to firm it up, or add more sugar, if desired.

When the cupcakes are cool, use a flat kitchen knife to help release them from the sides and bottom. Generously frost the cupcakes (you can frost the top only, or frost both the top and sides; there should be plenty of frosting). Sprinkle the top of the cupcakes with the finely chopped reserved walnuts and add a sliver or two of the sliced ginger on top. Serve immediately or loosely cover and refrigerate for up to 8 hours ahead of time.

55

# ❧ April ❧

# THE CHICKENS AND THE EGGS

The phone rang at 7 A.M., waking us from a deep slumber. It was our postmaster calling to tell us that a box had arrived and we needed to pick it up immediately. "It's making noises," she told us. John dressed quickly, ran down to the post office, and returned home clutching the box like a proud papa. Inside were twenty-five (two dozen, plus one "bonus") baby chicks, two days old, huddled together in clean sawdust, peeping vigorously. They looked like one big mass of baby pale-yellow feathers, using all their body heat to keep each other alive. We ordered the chicks through the mail because we wanted something more than the generic varieties our local feed store offers year after year. We wanted something exotic. And we got it.

Anconas, Barred Rocks, Redcaps, Silver Leghorns, and Minorcas were just some of the varieties we received. We still have most of that flock and they are stunning—white, black, red, light brown, dark brown, cream, and multicolored, long feathered and short.

Our chickens live well; they are often allowed to roam free, eat bugs (especially ticks), grass, and all the kitchen scraps we can give them. They seem to especially like beet peelings, heels of old French bread, and wilted, slightly soggy spinach and lettuce leaves.

In return they provide us with eggs that look like a child colored them for Easter but didn't bother to leave them in the dye long enough. They are the colors of a subdued rainbow — white, beige, tan, pale blue, turquoise, a subtle ocean green, and a strange almost forest green color. The yolks are brilliant sunflower yellow and the flavor is so pure and rich and deliciously eggy that I can't ever imagine eating commercially raised eggs at home again. Given the recent outbreaks of salmonella found in eggs, I think it's best if everyone find a small chicken farmer to buy their eggs from.

Despite cholesterol warnings from my physician, I have been cooking with lots of eggs. Deviled eggs. Egg salad. Cakes. Muffins. Soufflés. I have been whipping up frittatas and all types of omelets, but this morning's ultra-simple breakfast treat may be my new favorite egg dish of all. It's nothing more than an egg fried in hot olive oil (so much better than butter) and then drizzled with some fresh spring chive oil that you can whip up in a food processor or blender in a matter of minutes.

The yellow yolks, set off by the crispy brown edges of the egg whites (thanks to the olive oil) and the bright green chive oil is so gorgeous you may have troubling settling down and actually eating this dish. Crusty bread, lightly toasted and drizzled with some of the aforementioned chive oil, is a great addition. Oh, and strong coffee with steamed milk.

# Fried Eggs *in* Olive Oil *with* Fresh Chive Oil Drizzle

You know those people down the street with the chickens running around in their yard? Knock on the door and ask if they would be so kind as to sell you a dozen fresh eggs. It makes a huge difference. This is the ultimate breakfast treat, but it's also delicious for lunch or dinner. Place the fried eggs on top of fresh spring greens lightly dressed with olive oil and good wine vinegar, or sautéed spinach, kale, or chard, or even a bowl of steaming hot linguine.

*Serves 1 to 2*

> 1/2 **tablespoon olive oil**
> 2 **eggs**
> **sea salt and freshly ground black pepper**
> **chive oil (recipe follows)**
> **toast or crusty bread**

Heat a medium-size heavy skillet over moderate heat. Add the oil and let it get hot, 1 to 2 minutes. Add a speck of salt to test how hot the oil is; it should sizzle up. Carefully crack one egg into the pan and then the other. Let cook 1 to 2 minutes, or until the whites are set and the edges are just beginning to turn a golden, crispy brown. Drizzle about 1 teaspoon chive oil on top of each egg. Gently flip the eggs over, drizzle each egg with another teaspoon of chive oil, and cook another minute, depending on how runny or firm you like your yolks. Serve hot with toast or crusty bread drizzled with a touch more chive oil.

59

---

# Chive Oil

This oil will keep for a week or two covered and refrigerated. Drizzle over fried eggs, pasta, pizza, or seafood. It can also be added as a base to sauté meat, fish, or poultry.

*Makes about 1/2 cup*

> 1 **cup fresh chives, chopped**
> 1/2 **cup olive oil**
> **sea salt and freshly ground black pepper**

In a blender or food processor, blend the chives with the oil until almost smooth. The mixture will look like thick green oil. Season with salt and pepper to taste. Store the chive oil in a plastic squeeze bottle or a small covered jar.

# Roasted Spring Asparagus *with* Orange, Feta Cheese, *and* Poached Eggs

When we first bought our old farmhouse there were several asparagus plants that thrived despite serious neglect. Every year we got a dozen or so stalks, but one year deep in the woods behind the garden I discovered a patch of "wild" asparagus. This recipe was inspired by those fat, overgrown, early spring stalks. If you're making this dish for breakfast, serve it with crusty bread and home-fried sweet and white potatoes. If you're serving it for lunch or dinner, serve with a salad of mixed greens, crusty bread, and a good white wine.

*Serves 2 to 4*

> 1 pound fresh, local (or wild) asparagus, ends trimmed
> 2 tablespoons olive oil
> 1 teaspoon grated orange zest
> salt and freshly ground black pepper
> 4 eggs
> 1/2 cup crumbled feta cheese
> 1/4 cup minced fresh chives
> 4 slices crusty bread

Preheat the oven to 400 degrees.

Place the trimmed asparagus in a small roasting pan, ovenproof skillet, or shallow gratin dish and toss with 1 tablespoon of the oil, the orange zest, salt, and pepper. Roast for 12 to 20 minutes, depending on the thickness, or until the asparagus are *almost* tender when tested with a small sharp knife in the thickest part of the stalk. Be sure to toss the asparagus once or twice during the roasting time so they brown evenly. Remove from the oven *before* they are completely tender, as they will continue to cook in the hot pan after they've been taken out of the oven.

Meanwhile, bring a large skillet of water to a boil over high heat. Crack the eggs, one at a time, into the boiling water, reduce the heat to moderate, and let the eggs poach in the simmering water for 3 minutes for a really runny yolk and 4 minutes for a firmer yolk. Remove the eggs with a slotted spoon, being sure to let all the water drain.

Divide the asparagus between two or four plates and pour any pan juices on top. Sprinkle with the feta cheese and chives. Gently place one or two eggs on top of the asparagus and sprinkle with salt and pepper. Place one or two slices of bread next to the asparagus and eggs and pour the remaining olive oil on the toast.

# Garlic, Chive, *and* Saffron Aioli

Aioli, an egg-based, mayonnaise-like sauce used in French and Spanish dishes, is delicious when made with fresh eggs. Since the egg is not cooked, it's important that you know the source and trust the farmer. The yolk is whipped with garlic, chives, and a touch of saffron, and then thickened with the best olive oil you have in your pantry.

Saffron comes from the yellow-orange stigmas of a purple crocus, and is one of the most expensive spices in the world; but a little goes a long way in giving this sauce a gorgeous color and fragrance.

Make the aioli an hour or so before serving and keep it, covered, in the refrigerator. Serve with sautéed fish, shellfish, roast chicken, or as a dip for crusty bread served with salads. You can use this strongly flavored sauce in place of mayonnaise when you want a **strong** statement.

*Makes about ½ cup*

> 1 clove garlic, peeled and chopped
> ¼ teaspoon salt
> 1 pinch saffron, about ⅛ teaspoon
> 2 tablespoons finely minced chives
> 1 large egg yolk
> 1½ tablespoons lemon juice
> 1 tablespoon water
> ½ teaspoon Dijon mustard
> ½ cup olive oil
> freshly ground black pepper

In a medium bowl, mash the garlic and salt together using the back of spoon until it resembles a paste. Add the saffron and chives, and stir to mix it all together.

Using a hand whisk, add the egg yolk, lemon juice, water, and mustard and whisk vigorously. The idea is to add the olive oil in a very slow, steady stream, whisking the entire time. This is a great workout for your arms, but if you feel inclined, you can use a hand-held mixer with a whisk attachment on low. Whisk until all the oil is incorporated and the sauce is thickened. Taste for seasoning and add the pepper and more salt if needed.

Cover and refrigerate until ready to use — within a few hours.

# Meringue Cake *with* Vanilla Whipped Cream *and* Mixed Fruit

You don't want to use really fresh (day old) eggs for this meringue. Pick eggs that are at least 3 days old because the whites will whip up to produce a fuller, airier meringue. This is a tough recipe to follow on a humid summer day. Meringue hates humidity, but it's so delicious served with mixed summer berries that it's hard to resist in the summer months. In the winter you can fill the cake with chopped apples, pears, bananas, mangoes, and other winter fruit.

*Serves 6*

### For the meringue:

6 egg whites
1/8 teaspoon cream of tartar
3/4 cup sugar
1 cup confectioners' sugar

### For the filling:

1 1/2 cups heavy cream
2 tablespoons sugar
1/2 teaspoon vanilla extract
4 cups fruit, mixed berries or any thinly sliced combination of fresh fruit

Preheat the oven to 250 degrees. Line two cookie sheets with parchment paper, using a touch of butter directly on the cookie sheets to make sure the paper sticks to the pan. Turn a large (12-inch) bowl upside down and trace a 12-inch circle onto the parchment paper in pencil. Repeat on the second sheet of parchment.

In a mixing bowl, beat the egg whites and cream of tartar for about 2 minutes on medium, or until soft peaks form. Add the granulated sugar and beat another 4 minutes, on medium, until the whites are glossy white and firm. Remove from the mixer and gently fold in the confectioners' sugar with a spoon or soft spatula, making sure there are no clumps of sugar.

Using a spoon, scoop half the meringue into the 12-inch circle on the parchment paper. Using the back of a metal spoon or a soft spatula, make a slight depression in the center of the circle so that the sides are higher than the center. (This will be where you will fill in the whipped cream and fruit; it will be easier to spoon the fruit in the center of the meringue if there is a dip in the center.) Repeat with the remaining meringue on the other cookie sheet.

Place in the oven on the top and middle shelves, and reduce the temperature to 225 degrees. Bake for 1 hour. Reverse the cookie sheets and bake another hour. Depending on the weather, the meringue should feel firm (with no mushy, soft feeling when you press down gently on it). If you're making this in the summer, chances are good you'll need to bake the meringue for about 3 hours. Cool in the oven until room temperature. Remove and let cool.

To make the filling, whip the cream until almost stiff. Add the sugar and the vanilla and whip until stiff.

Carefully peel the largest meringue layer from the parchment paper and place on the bottom of a cake plate. Add half the cream in the center and fill in with half the fruit. Gently peel the second layer off the parchment and place it on top of the cream and fruit, gently pressing down. Add the remaining cream in the center and add the remaining fruit on top. Serve cold.

The meringue layers can be cooled, covered in plastic, and refrigerated overnight. Do not assemble the cake until several hours before serving.

# WILD THINGS,
# I THINK I LOVE YOU: RAMPS

**W**e set out early, heavily anointed with bug spray, sensibly dressed in long pants, socks, and good hiking shoes, but still we couldn't fight off the mosquitoes. It was the last day of April, early morning, overcast, humid, and those bugs were out in force. You know that television ad where they spray a man with super-hairy arms with a strong, toxic bug repellent and then leave the other arm unsprayed, and he puts his arms in a box full of mosquitoes and you watch them swarm on his unsprayed arm? Well my entire body felt like that unsprayed arm.

Still, I was upbeat. We were on an early morning hike in search of the elusive ramp, or wild leek. For the past month my friend Hope and I, who walk our dogs in the woods near our house virtually every morning, had become *obsessed* with finding ramps. They were in our local specialty vegetable store (at close to twenty dollars a pound), but we were determined to find them in the wild.

Obsession sounds like an exaggeration, a word chosen for dramatic impact. But I am really talking about true, blown-out obsession. Every day, on every walk, we talked about ramps the way most women talk about their children. We were sure the small green leaf unfurling near the stream in the nearby woods was a ramp. Nope. We were sure we would find them near the river, in a woody, hilly area. Nope. And when the weather suddenly turned hot, into the 1980s in mid-April, we were sure they'd shoot up through the leaves in the woods. Nope. I spent hours researching on the Web, looking at pictures of ramps in their various stages. I even went so far as to buy half a pound of ramps at the vegetable store, shove them under my dog's nose, and try to train her to find them like a truffle-hunting pig in the Italian countryside. "Chloe, ramps! Ramps, Chloe. Go find them, girl."

Hope said she had a friend who knew where to find ramps. Like every other forager I've met, this friend was adamant that we not use her real name, or tell our exact location. So let's just call the friend "Julie," and let's just say we were somewhere south of Portland. That's it. I can't tell you more. (You might try asking Chloe to lead you there.)

Three women, three dogs, three thousand mosquitoes. We walked through the woods, following a trail until Julie said "No! Down here!" and led us off trail and down steep terrain towards a stream and a small pool of collected rainwater. We bushwhacked along this area for about ten minutes and then I saw a huge patch of gorgeous, oval-shaped green leaves streaked with white and pale pink stripes down the center. I was in shock. All that talk, all those walks, all those misguided schleps through the woods, all those blackflies and mosquitoes, and finally we had arrived at what appeared to be a field dotted with thousands of ramps.

They were buried under rocks and near rocks, like chickens hiding from a fox. They seemed to favor the moist, shady area, with sandy soil. Although much of my research told me to hunt in sloped areas, this ramp patch was on a perfectly flat piece of land, right near a stream. We found them covered in leaves and mulch, their smooth green leaves popping through the brown earth. They weren't all that easy to pull up and, for some strange reason, we hadn't thought to bring shovels or bags or tools of any kind. I think we never really believed we would find them, that somehow we had made all this up. As if ramps, or *Allium trioccum*, were simply a figment of our imagination.

If you're out foraging and not sure you've got a ramp (and, like me, you worry about picking something dangerously inedible), you simply need to pull one up and snip off a piece of the leaf. If your nose is not assaulted by the strong scent of onion then you don't have a ramp. (A member of the lily family, a ramp's leaves resemble a longer, wider, more elegant lily of the valley.) And when you pull ramps out of the ground, you'll discover white, scallion-like bulbs covered in thin brown skin.

We picked quickly and intensely, barely talking. Within fifteen minutes I had an armload of ramps — I figured around one hundred dollars worth at an upscale market — and an entire mosquito population intimately getting to know my arms and neck. There were so many ramp patches we could have easily filled a large suitcase, sold them in town, and paid off some serious bills. But we tried not to be greedy. As soon as we got back on the trail to head home, the skies opened up and the rain came down, but it didn't matter. You think a kid leaving a candy store with a bag full of treats cares about a little rain? That's how it felt. We were drenched in the oncoming storm, coated in bugs, and I, for one, couldn't have been happier.

Your first taste will be something you're likely to remember for a long time. When raw, ramps have an overwhelming smell, like a cross between wild onions and dirty socks. They don't whisper. They scream, "Here I am, just try and ignore me." But cooking transforms ramps into a delicacy. Imagine taking a leek, a clove of garlic, a sweet Vidalia-type onion, a scallion, and a shallot, putting them all into a machine and extracting the single most distinguishing flavor element from each.

According to the late R.W. Apple, Jr., writing in the *New York Times* (April 2003), "The origin of the name is in dispute. Most authorities, including the Department of Agriculture, consider 'ramp' a shortened form of 'ramsom,' which is an old name for the European counterpart of the ramp, *Allium ursinum,* or bear garlic. 'Ramson' is

65

thought by some to come from the Old English word for wild leeks, *hramsen*, and by others, of a more romantic cast of mind, to denote 'son of ram,' Aries being the sign under which ramps appear."

I cleaned my stash of ramps well under cold running water, picking out pine needles and crumpled leaves. I pulled the brown skin off the bulbs and dried them off. Then I set out to work. I spent close to two weeks cooking with the ramps; I fried the leaves and bulbs in olive oil in a hot skillet for 5 minutes, and then fried a few eggs on top *(page 59)*; I pureed a batch and cooked them with sweet sea scallops *(page 69)*; I made a French-style tart with ramps and spring mushrooms *(pages 70–71)*; I tried a grilled cheese and ramp sandwich; I grilled them over a charcoal fire with olive oil, sea salt, and freshly ground black pepper; I made an exceptional ramp pesto; I sautéed them and then chopped them up finely and mixed them with butter *(page 68)* to create ramp "garlic" bread. Ramps can dress up even the most basic food. A little wild leek made everything that came out of my kitchen taste better than ever.

# Ramp Puree

You can use this puree in the scallop recipe that follows, or add it to the skillet when you're sautéing a steak, pork chop, lamb, or seafood. It adds a good kick of flavor to vinaigrettes, stews, soups, or as a flavor base for pizza. Or make this simple crostini: spread a generous teaspoon of ramp puree on a slice of crusty bread. Place under the broiler for a minute. Sprinkle with a generous teaspoon of grated Parmesan cheese and broil another minute, or until the cheese is bubbling.

*Makes about ½ cup*

> 5 ounces ramps, well washed, ends trimmed, and skin removed from
>      the white bulb, chopped
> 3 tablespoons olive oil
> sea salt and freshly ground black pepper

Bring a medium-size pot of water to boil over high heat. Add the ramps and cook for 2 minutes; drain under cold running water and drain again, making sure all the water is removed.

Place the drained ramps in a food processor or blender and add the olive oil. Blend until thick and chunky. Remove to a small bowl and season to taste with the salt and pepper. The puree can be covered and refrigerated for a day.

# Ramp Butter

This is a great way to extend the ramp season. The ramps are sautéed lightly in olive oil and then pureed with butter. The gorgeous green butter is bursting with fresh ramp flavor and is fabulous melted over a grilled steak, grilled or sautéed seafood, or used like you would garlic butter to make garlic bread. Try a grilled cheese and ramp butter sandwich. You can also use this instead of garlic butter when making Roasted Garlic Bread *(page 176)*.

*Makes about ½ cup*

>    2 tablespoons olive oil
>    5 ounces fresh ramps, well washed, ends trimmed, and skin removed from
>       the white bulb, with the white scallion-like bulb separated and left whole,
>       and greens coarsely chopped
>    salt and freshly ground black pepper
>    1 stick lightly salted butter, at room temperature

Heat the oil in a large skillet over moderate heat. Add the white scallion-like bulbs of the ramps and sauté, stirring occasionally, for 5 minutes. Season with salt and pepper. Remove from the heat and add the greens and stir.

Place the still warm ramps and the oil from the skillet into the container of a food processor or blender. Add the stick of butter and pulse until the butter softens (it may even melt from the heat of the ramps) and the ramps are fully incorporated. Place the butter into 1 or 2 ramekins and refrigerate for up to 4 days, or cover and freeze for up to 3 months.

### Tip

*Scallions can be substituted for ramps, but they are much subtler. Add a clove of chopped garlic as well.*

# Sautéed Sea Scallops *with* Ramp Puree *and* Sautéed Whole Ramps

The sweetness of scallops marries well with the assertive nature of ramps. And the bright green ramp color really adds a nice touch to the neutral white scallops.

*Serves 4*

> 2 tablespoons olive oil
> 6 whole ramps, well washed, ends trimmed, and skin removed from white
>     bulb, left whole
> ¾ cup flour
> salt and freshly ground black pepper
> 1 pound fresh sea scallops, very lightly rinsed and thoroughly dried
> 4 tablespoons Ramp Puree, *(page 67)*
> ¾ cup dry white wine

Preheat the oven to 300 degrees.

Prepare the scallops: in a large skillet heat ½ tablespoon of the oil over high heat. Add the whole ramps and cook 1 minute per side, until the greens "puff" up and the white scallion-like bulb is tender. Remove and set aside.

Place the flour on a small plate and season liberally with the salt and pepper. Very lightly dredge the scallops in the seasoned flour, making sure to coat them on all sides.

Heat the remaining oil in the large skillet over high heat. Add the scallops to the hot oil and cook 2 minutes, without disturbing them. Gently flip the scallops over and cook another minute. Add 3 tablespoons of the ramp puree to the pan and, using a soft spatula, stir the puree around to coat all the scallops. Cook another minute and remove the scallops to a serving plate and keep warm in the preheated oven.

Keep the skillet over high heat and add the wine, scraping up any bits clinging to the bottom. Cook about 4 minutes, or until the wine is reduced slightly. Stir in another tablespoon of the ramp puree and the sautéed whole ramps and cook another minute. Pour the hot sauce and the whole ramps over the scallops and garnish the top of the dish with the cooked whole ramps.

# Ramp *and* **Mushroom Tart**

If you can find wild spring morels, this French-style tart bursts with the flavors of the spring woods. Or you can use crimini mushrooms or your favorite variety of wild mushroom. Serve with a salad of spring greens and a lightly sparkling white wine.

*Serves 4 to 6*

### *For the pastry:*

1¹/₂ cups flour
1 pinch salt
1¹/₂ sticks unsalted butter, chilled and cut into small pieces
¹/₃ cup ice cold water

### *For the tart:*

2 tablespoons olive oil
1 large Vidalia onion, thinly sliced
salt and freshly ground black pepper
8¹/₂ ounces ramps, ends trimmed and skin removed from the white bulb,
      with the bulb and greens chopped
7 ounces morels or crimini mushrooms, or wild local spring mushrooms,
      ends trimmed and thickly sliced
2 eggs
³/₄ cup heavy cream
1 cup grated Gruyere cheese
¹/₂ cup grated Parmesan cheese

In the container of a food processor, whirl the flour and salt. Add the butter and pulse about 15 times, or until the butter is the size of coarse cornmeal. With the motor running, add enough cold water until the dough *just* begins to come together and pull away from the sides of the machine. Remove the dough and place in plastic wrap and chill for at least an hour.

Make the filling in a large skillet. Heat 1¹/₂ tablespoons of the oil over low heat. Add the onion and cook, stirring frequently, for 8 minutes. Season with salt and pepper. Add the ramps and cook, stirring frequently, for 5 minutes. Add the remaining oil and the mushrooms and cook another 5 minutes, stirring once or twice. Remove from the heat and let cool.

In a large bowl, whisk together the eggs with a pinch of salt and pepper. Whisk in the cream and then stir in the two cheeses.

Remove the pastry from the refrigerator. Working on a well-floured surface, roll out the dough to fit an 11 x 8 inch rectangular tart pan or 9-inch round tart pan with a removable bottom. Trim the excess pastry off the edges and discard. Poke a few holes in the bottom and sides of the pastry with the tines of a fork. Chill.

Preheat the oven to 350 degrees.

Place the crust in the preheated oven for 10 minutes. Remove from the oven. Raise the oven temperature to 400 degrees.

Pour the cooled ramp mixture into the egg mixture, stirring well. Place the filling in the prepared pastry and bake on the middle shelf for 30 minutes. Reduce the heat to 325 degrees and continue baking for another 20 minutes, or until the filling turns a light golden brown, and a toothpick inserted in the center comes out dry. Let cool for a few minutes and then cut into serving pieces. Serve hot or at room temperature.

---

### ➤ Fiddleheads ◄

*"If I tell you where I gather my fiddleheads," a man from Down East told me, only half joking, "I'm afraid I'll have to hurt you." This kind of "protective spirit" is common throughout Maine. I suppose gold diggers and Italian truffle hunters feel this way, not letting anyone know where they take their pigs to sniff out the elusive and highly valuable truffle. But an ostrich fern? Fiddlehead ferns don't sell for nearly a quarter of the price of gold, or a truffle, and are abundant in April and May throughout New England — if you know where to find them.*

*Named for its resemblance to the scroll of a violin, or fiddle, fiddleheads are the young, edible, tightly coiled fronds of the ostrich (also called pothole) fern. Whether you find your fiddleheads by a river (in the dark of night with no one looking) or at the grocery store (it's one of the few local wild foods supermarkets seem to carry faithfully each spring), choose ones that are tightly curled, firm, bright green, and compact. The skin or scale that covers the coiled fern, called the "chaff," is another gauge of freshness. When fiddleheads have just been harvested, the scale or skin will be a green color, which browns as it ages. The best way to remove this skin is to rub it briskly between your hands.*

*I love the clean, fresh, slightly wild asparagus flavor of fiddleheads and am not big on cooking then with a lot of other flavors. My favorite technique? Simply blanche the fiddleheads in boiling water for a minute or two, drain them under cold running water, drain again, and then sauté them in hot olive oil with garlic.*

# Linguine *with* Maine Clam Sauce, Ramps, *and* Garlic

This is my take on classic Italian clam sauce, where whole clams are sautéed with garlic and olive oil and then steamed open in the shell in white wine. The addition of fresh ramps, sautéed with the garlic, is really interesting — a wild onion flavor and a great green color infuse the clams and the sauce.

Serve on top of a pound of cooked linguine or spaghetti, or on its own with crusty bread (the juices are just too good to waste a single drop).

*Serves 4*

> 1 pound linguine or spaghetti
> 3 tablespoons olive oil
> 3 cloves garlic, chopped
> 3 ounces ramps, well washed, ends trimmed and white skin removed from
>     white bulb, chopped
> 1 pinch chile flakes
> freshly ground black pepper
> 2 to 2½ pounds Maine littleneck or mahogany clams, scrubbed clean
> 1⅓ cups dry white wine
> sea salt, optional

Bring a pot of water to a boil for the pasta. Cook a pound of linguine, if desired.

Meanwhile, make the sauce. In a large skillet, heat the oil over high heat. Add the garlic and half the ramps, a small pinch of chile flakes, and a grinding of black pepper. Cook for 10 seconds. Add the clams and cook, stirring to make sure they are coated in the oil and garlic and ramps, and cook 1 minute. Add the wine and let it come to a boil on high heat, reduce the heat to low, and let simmer about 5 minutes, stirring frequently. Taste the sauce; add a pinch of salt if needed and additional pepper and chile flakes if desired. Cover the skillet and cook another few minutes or until the clams are opened and the sauce is reduced enough not to taste too much of the wine. If the sauce tastes too winey, remove the clams with a slotted spoon and continue to reduce the sauce for another 3 to 5 minutes. Add the clams back to the skillet.

Pour on top of the cooked, drained pasta, or serve from the skillet with crusty bread.

# May

# MOTHER'S DAY TRADITIONS

My older daughter writes, in an email from Beijing, China, where she is living and working, that she and several of her twenty-something ex-pat friends have been getting together to have cooking competitions, inspired by the hugely popular television shows *Top Chef* and *Iron Chef*. "We had our first Tron (Top meets Iron) chef competition on Friday and I won! The secret ingredient was pomelo [a Southeast Asian citrus fruit]. I made enchiladas with pomelo salsa and Vietnamese noodle salad with pomelo dressing. It was pretty delicious, if I do say so myself. I wanted to make a pomelo lassi, but we don't have a blender."

My younger daughter texts from her college dorm: "Cooking with friends tonight. Making chicken piccata. Is there a substitute for wine that I can use when I deglaze the skillet?"

It makes a mother proud. Two girls growing up in the kitchen of a food writer who wanted so desperately to fit in with the other kids who ate "normal" food. When they were little I would get "the look" when I suggested our leftovers — sushi, homemade Asian dumplings, vegetable soups with pesto, roast chicken with lemon, stir-fried spicy tofu — go into their school lunch box the next day. "Mom, it's so embarrassing! If I brought sushi to the cafeteria, I would get made fun of *so bad!*"

On the few occasions that I visited the school at lunchtime, I was shocked at what kids were eating. There were peanut butter and jelly sandwiches on squishy white bread with boxes of purple and pink sugary juice and candy bars. But, even worse, the majority of the first and second graders were eating out of plastic containers with little dividers where processed cheese sat next to processed meat, which sat next to processed cookies or pudding. Keep in mind this was before Alice Waters started talking about the importance of healthy school lunches, and a full decade before a major television network offered a show about a chef trying to revolutionize the way a small town eats. In some cases it was an economic choice that led parents to send their kids to school with these popular, pre-made, inexpensive lunches, but in many other cases it was simply a matter of convenience for working parents with little time to shop and cook.

"No way," I told my girls as we walked through the supermarket and one of them spotted a cute cartoon character on top of the bologna lunch trays. "Oh, Mom, come on," they wailed. "Everyone eats this stuff. It's really good! You should try it!" This was one point on which I refused to waver. They could have dresses with cartoon characters or T-shirts with slogans, but no bologna sealed in a plastic tray. If memory serves me well, I challenged them right there in the supermarket. "So, if everyone jumped off the bridge, would you jump, too?" Groan. Groan. The pitiable daughters of a food writer.

Birthday parties were the most telling times. Generally we had small family dinners (with one highly trusted best friend) and the girls were allowed to choose the menu. Dinners on these occasions ranged from escargot with garlic butter, the aforementioned roast chicken with lemon and herbs, shepherd's pie, mashed potatoes with roasted garlic, homemade sushi, Chinese mapo doufu, baked goat cheese with tomatoes, chocolate mousse served in parfait cups layered with fresh berries and real whipped cream, and homemade birthday cakes. But when the girls' friends came over for the big "public" birthday party, we ordered pizza from the local take-out and served frozen ice cream cake from the grocery store. I was mostly okay with this because I figured if ordering pizza and cake was all it took for them to feel part of something, then things could be a whole lot worse. It became clear over the years that the girls had very definitive ideas about what was acceptable "public food," in contrast to the private, homemade, adventurous foods they ate at home each night.

Now they are grown, out in the world taking food and their daily diet into their own hands. And according to recent emails and text messages, food and cooking have become a way for them to entertain, and show friends that they grew up in a house where food was understood and appreciated. Goat cheese, ginger, and lemongrass are out of the closet. I always believed that this time would come, but it's still a pleasant surprise.

Every May, whether the girls are here or calling me from a far-flung spot in the world to wish me a happy Mother's Day, I am flooded with memories of the Mother's Day breakfasts they cooked each year. Remembering those little girls walking upstairs to my bedroom with breakfast on a tray are among my best memories of their childhoods. "Close your eyes, Mommy. We have a really special treat." And then the burst of song, to the tune of *Happy Birthday*, "Happy Mother's Day Dear Mommy..." We would nestle the tray among the sheets and quilts and they would snuggle in next to me, presumably to watch me eat my special meal in bed, but within minutes one would ask for a bite of the fruit, and then the eggs, until...whoops, no food left on the tray. "Sorry, Mommy. We ate your Mother's Day Breakfast."

Mother's Day Sunday meant the girls would rise "early" — as little kids that often meant the crack of dawn, but as pre-teens and teenagers, alarm clocks were set for eleven so the meal served just before noon could still officially be called "breakfast." Together with John's assistance, they would take over the kitchen and claim it as their own for this one day. They would divide up the chores. One went outside and cut little blossoms off the just-flowering trees and placed them in a small, always wobbly vase. The other would whip the eggs and choose the filling for the omelets or the scramble. There was almost always smoked salmon, bagels, cream cheese, and a fruit salad with the first real strawberries of the year, along with whatever other fruit happened to be in the kitchen.

I would lie in bed, supposedly luxuriating, surrounded by the Sunday paper. But the truth is I would lie there listening to the sounds of my family doing something for me. Often, almost every year in fact, there was fighting. Sometimes screaming, yelling fights. "No, Maya, you got to make the omelets last year. It's my turn." Or, "Emma, you did it all wrong. That's not the right way to cut basil." Lying there year after year, May's early birds chirping and the sun coming in through the bedroom windows, I understood that, despite their protests about how "weird" the food in our house was, they were watching and listening when their father and I cooked dinner every night. How else would they know what a loving touch it was when they sprinkled fresh garden chives and their fuzzy pink flowers on top of the white cream cheese? Or know to take a strawberry and a slice of orange and cut thin slits in them so they balance along the edge of the glass of orange juice as sweet, colorful garnishes? Or sprinkle fresh chopped mint into the fruit salad to bring out the sweetness?

As they got older the breakfast dishes became more sophisticated. Several years ago, Emma presented me with a smoked salmon Benedict with artichoke-caper-lemon butter—no recipe to follow, she just whipped it up in under an hour on Mother's Day morning *(pages 78–79)*.

For my daughters, food was an obsession that often embarrassed them. When Emma was young she would say things like, "Why can't we just be like *normal* people and have plain old food? Why does everything have to be so *fancy*?" She would come home from play dates thrilled at her amazing new discovery of "macaroni and cheese from a box." I was wise enough not to push things. "Who wants to cook with me?" I would ask. But the girls were always too busy riding horses, acting in school plays, reading books, hanging out with friends, and playing softball.

There were many years, particularly on holidays, when I would grow resentful as I cooked without their help. "If I dropped dead tomorrow," I would snap at them, "would you guys know how to make Thanksgiving/Passover/Chanukah/Christmas dinner?" We celebrated pretty much everything when the girls were little because, the way I figured it, every holiday was an excuse for a feast and that meant more cooking and more time around the family table. "We'd figure it out if we had to," Maya answered, knowing at a young age how to appease me. They would snip the ends off green beans and clean spinach and break bread into small pieces for stuffing, but I always imagined that at least one of them would be there, glued to my side, wanting to learn every step of the meal. Would they really know how to make creamed spinach *(page 82)* with just the right amount of nutmeg? Would they know to add seltzer to the matzo balls instead of plain water to make them fluffy and light? Would they know that every year, when no one was looking, I chopped a dozen fresh oysters with their liquor and stirred them into the bread and celery stuffing before placing it inside the turkey?

These recent emails from the girls about cooking for entertainment in a tiny, ill-equipped kitchen in Beijing, and making meals with new friends in a college apartment came as part revelation and part relief. The girls certainly don't have to embrace food as a profession or even, to use their word, as an "obsession." But it sure was good to learn that they understand how relaxing and bonding cooking can be. It's good to know that one day, when they have families of their own, they might remember that rosemary and garlic cloves go into the chicken cavity along with a whole lemon and that the chicken starts off roasting at 450 degrees for 30 minutes to develop a crisp skin, and is then reduced to 350 degrees. It's good to know that, even though they didn't appear to care all that much about cooking and what I was doing every day, they really were watching closely.

# Emma's Spinach *and* Smoked-Salmon Benedict *with* Artichoke-Caper-Lemon Butter

Emma's recipe omits the heavy bacon and hollandaise sauce traditionally served with eggs Benedict and replaces them with smoked salmon, baby spinach, and a light sauce made with artichoke hearts, capers, and fresh lemon juice mixed with a touch of butter. Serve with hot coffee, or iced tea, and a spring fruit salad.

*Serves 2 to 4*

### For the sauce:

4 tablespoons unsalted butter
1/2 cup jarred artichoke hearts, drained and chopped
1/4 cup capers, drained
1 pinch sea salt
freshly ground black pepper
1 tablespoon fresh lemon juice
1 teaspoon grated lemon zest

### For the eggs:

1 tablespoon olive oil
1 cup packed baby spinach
salt and freshly ground black pepper
2 English muffins, or whole-wheat English muffins, or four 1-inch-thick
    slices of your favorite bread
4 large eggs
8 thin slices smoked salmon

Melt the butter in a small saucepan. Add the artichokes, capers, just a touch of salt, pepper, lemon juice, and lemon zest and cook for two minutes. Set aside or keep warm over very low heat.

In a medium skillet, heat the oil over moderately high heat. Add the spinach and stir until wilted, 2 to 3 minutes. Season with salt and pepper. Keep warm over very low heat.

Bring 4 cups of water to a boil in a separate medium skillet.

Separate the muffins and place in the toaster.

When the water is boiling, reduce the heat to moderate so the water is at a gentle simmer. Crack the eggs into a bowl, one at a time, and add to the skillet. Cook about 3 minutes, depending on how firm you like your poached eggs. This will result in a runny yolk and firm whites.

Toast the muffin until golden brown. Place a muffin half (or 2 muffin halves) on two to four plates and top each with two slices of salmon, making sure they overlap the muffin slightly so you'll see the color once the egg goes on top. Divide the spinach between each muffin half and place on the salmon.

Warm the Artichoke–Caper–Lemon butter over low heat. Drain the eggs well and place one on each muffin. Spoon 1 to 2 tablespoons of the warm butter on top and serve hot.

---

# Maya's Fruit Salad *with* Blood Orange Juice *and* Mint

This is the classic Mother's Day fruit salad the girls made for me year after year. You can use any variety of fresh fruit, but be sure to try the orange juice and fresh mint to add an extra dimension of flavor.

*Serves 4*

> 1 pineapple, skin and core removed
> 1 cantaloupe, rind and seeds removed
> 1 banana, peeled
> 1 cup strawberries (hulled), raspberries, and/or blackberries
> 3 tablespoons chopped fresh mint, plus 4 mint leaves left whole
> 1/3 cup freshly squeezed, blood orange juice, regular orange juice,
>     or orange juice with pulp

Cut the pineapple and melon into 1-inch pieces. Cut the banana into 1-inch pieces. Place the pineapple and melon in a bowl and add the banana slices. Sprinkle on the berries, chopped mint, and orange juice and mix gently. Garnish with fresh mint leaves. Cover and refrigerate until ready to serve.

# Roast Chicken *with* Lemon, Rosemary, *and* Garlic

This is a family classic. I roasted some variation of this chicken at least once a week when the kids were growing up. I love this dish because it's pure comfort food and it never goes wrong. You can surround the chicken with potatoes, carrots, leeks, onions, parsnips, baby turnips, or any other favorite root vegetables.

*Serves 4*

    1 lemon, scored in several places
    one (3- to 4-pound) roasting chicken, rinsed and excess fat removed
    8 cloves garlic, peeled and left whole
    3 tablespoons fresh rosemary, chopped
    1 cup red or white wine
    1½ tablespoons olive oil
    salt and freshly ground black pepper
    1 tablespoon fresh thyme, chopped
    sweet Hungarian paprika
    4 medium potatoes, peeled and each potato cut into four pieces

Preheat the oven to 450 degrees.

Place the lemon inside the cavity along with a clove of garlic and 1 tablespoon of the rosemary. Cut a small piece of kitchen twine and tie the legs together using a small, simple knot. Remove any excess string. Tuck the wings under the bird (this avoids them getting burnt). Place the chicken in a large roasting pan or gratin dish.

Pour the wine on top of the chicken. Pour half the olive oil on top of the bird and sprinkle with salt, pepper, half the remaining rosemary, and half the thyme. Sprinkle liberally with paprika. Place on the middle shelf and roast for 30 minutes.

Place the potatoes in a bowl and add the remaining oil, rosemary, thyme, salt, and pepper and toss to coat thoroughly.

Remove the chicken from the oven and place the potatoes (and any other vegetables you may be using) around the bird. Reduce the temperature to 350 degrees, and roast for another 45 minutes to an hour, basting the bird several times and tossing the potatoes and vegetables.

Remove the bird from the oven and make sure the juices run yellow and not pink when you pierce the inside of the leg with a small sharp knife. Test the potatoes and make sure they are tender throughout. Let sit for 5 minutes. Remove the string and carve the bird. Serve hot with the potatoes and the pan juices.

# Garlic Mashed Potatoes

Like most families, we *love* mashed potatoes. They are even better when you add a whole head of roasted garlic cloves. I've given a range for the amount of butter, milk, and/or cream you can use in this recipe, depending on just how rich, creamy, and decadent you want the dish to be.

*Serves 6*

10 to 14 cloves garlic, peeled and left whole
2 tablespoons olive oil
salt and freshly ground black pepper
3 pounds medium Yukon Gold potatoes, peeled and cut in half
3 to 4 tablespoons unsalted butter
1 to 1 1/2 cups low-fat or whole milk
1/2 to 3/4 cup heavy cream, optional

Preheat the oven to 325 degrees. Place the peeled garlic cloves in a small ovenproof skillet, or shallow casserole, and toss with the olive oil, salt, and pepper. Roast on the middle shelf for about 12 minutes, or until the cloves are tender and a pale golden brown. If they look like they are burning or getting too brown, reduce the temperature to 300 and cover loosely with aluminum foil.

Meanwhile, bring a large pot of water to a rolling boil over high heat. Add the potatoes and cook for 20 to 25 minutes, or until the potatoes feel tender when tested in the center with a small, sharp knife. Drain the potatoes thoroughly.

Place the potatoes back into the pot over very low heat. Add the butter and, using a potato masher, mash the potatoes, working in the butter. (Alternatively, use a ricer to puree the potatoes, place them back into the pot, and then add the butter.) Add the roasted garlic cloves and the oil from the pan and mash them into the potatoes.

Slowly add the milk and cream (if using), mashing and stirring. I am not of the mashed-potatoes-must-be-smooth school, so don't stress if there are still some lumps. Add salt and pepper to taste and add additional milk and cream as needed.

# Creamed Spinach *with* Yogurt *and* Nutmeg

This recipe has a long legacy in our family, beginning with my father, who never loved vegetables but adored creamed spinach. During the holidays we make it with heavy cream and freshly ground nutmeg — over the years I've lightened it up a bit. Instead of heavy cream I substitute local yogurt or a thick Greek-style yogurt. If you don't have either of those, you can take plain yogurt and place it in a tightly meshed sieve for an hour or so, until much of the liquid is released and drained and you're left with a thick yogurt mixture. Look for whole nutmeg and a little nutmeg grater (or you can use the very tiny holes on a box cheese grater); it makes a huge difference. You can easily double or triple the recipe to serve a larger crowd.

*Serves 4*

> 2 1/2 tablespoons olive oil
> 1 pound fresh spinach or baby spinach, washed and thoroughly dried (if stems
>   are very thick and long they can be removed)
> 2 to 3 cloves garlic, finely chopped
> salt and freshly ground black pepper
> 1/4 to 1/2 teaspoon freshly ground nutmeg
> 1/2 cup yogurt

In a large skillet, heat 1/2 tablespoon of the oil over high heat. Add half the spinach and cook, stirring, for 2 to 3 minutes, or until wilted but not necessarily cooked through. Remove to a chopping board. Add another tablespoon of the oil and sauté the remaining spinach in the same manner; remove to the chopping board.

Chop the spinach (some like it finely chopped and others coarsely chopped).

Add the remaining 1 tablespoon of the oil to the skillet over moderate heat. Add the garlic and cook, stirring, for about 10 seconds. Add the chopped spinach, salt, pepper, and nutmeg, stirring well, and cook 1 minute. Add the yogurt, stirring it into the spinach, and let cook over low heat for about 5 minutes, or until slightly thickened and hot. Taste for seasoning, adding more salt, pepper, or nutmeg if needed. (The spinach can be served hot from the skillet or placed in a small casserole and refrigerated for several hours. Place in a preheated 350 degree oven for about 12 minutes, or until bubbling and hot throughout.)

*Tip*

*You can also add all kinds of different spices: add a dash of cardamom, allspice, chile flakes, or cayenne.*

# ≋ June ≋

# FIRST TASTES OF SUMMER

There was a game we used to play as kids: If you were stuck on a desert island and could only have one type of food, what would it be? My answer has changed frequently over the years—from hot dogs to fried chicken to crepes to tacos to roast chicken to anything with goat cheese, and, more recently, from dumplings to Korean pork buns. But I'm pretty sure I know my final answer. I want a salad. Not just any salad, but one from my garden, a simple mix of greens, lightly dressed with fragrant olive oil, wine vinegar, sea salt, and freshly ground black pepper. That's it.

If that sounds pretentious or, even, insane, you haven't tasted the greens from my garden. In June, when the new greens are plentiful enough to fill the salad bowl for the first time, I gather a few leaves of each variety. There's mache, arugula, green and red oakleaf, buttercrunch, beautiful Lollo Rossa, and mustard greens. I throw in some shredded basil leaves (tiny and barely formed), chopped chives, and parsley. The bowl is filled with red- and green-tinged leaves. There are smooth surfaces and rough ones, ruffled and jagged. But it's the explosion of taste that really matters.

Close your eyes and taste a forkful of greens. I mean *really* taste. There, you get the pepper and biting flavor of the arugula and purple-tinged mizuna, a Japanese mustard green, and the pleasing way it creeps down your throat subtly at first and then with a wham at the end. The buttercrunch lettuce, sweet and easy, has a happy summer green flavor and a good crunch. Juicy, spicy, crunchy, chewy, tender — all these flavors and textures erupting in your mouth. And, there's not an ounce of guilt. These greens are nothing but good for you.

That same sensation, of tasting food in an intense, new way, can be said for the first strawberries, peas, beans, tomatoes, zucchini, or virtually anything you grow yourself. This is, after all, the primary reason to grow a garden. To experience that just-picked fresh flavor from fruits and vegetables. Every time I meet a parent who tells me their child won't eat fruits or vegetables, I tell them to grow a garden or visit a pick-your-own farm. It's hard for any kid, or adult for that matter, to eat a strawberry, warm from the sun, fresh from the vine, juice dripping down their chin, and not admit it's pretty delicious.

Last winter I visited the Museum of Fine Arts in Boston and spent hours wandering the galleries. In one room filled with French impressionists, I zoomed in on a single painting. I don't recall the artist, or the year, but I can tell you, in vivid detail, about the subject. There was a long table with many jolly, slightly drunk-looking French men and women, seated in chairs around it. Situated in a beautiful field in the countryside, this table overflowed with platters of meats, bowls of fruit, cheeses, bread, jugs of wine. The just-flowering tree branches provided shade and everyone looked happy and relaxed.

Inside that hushed gallery, with its artificial light and pumped in heat, I wanted nothing more than to jump inside that scene. I made a vow to have a twenty-first-century version of that party come June.

I will set up several long tables in the field just beyond my house. I will pick any and everything available in my garden and augment it with fruit and vegetables from the farmer's market. I will invite food-loving friends to come with their own best-of-June food and many bottles of wine and toast the season in style.

I imagine huge bowls of just-picked peas, a cold or hot soup (depending on the weather; *page 88*), bowls of local strawberries, Maine-made cheeses, crusty breads, bottles of wine, and a sense of deep celebration. I will give the mosquitoes and black-flies the day off, and order up cool, gentle breezes, a not-too-hot sun, and brilliant blue skies. It will be a perfect June afternoon with fresh, local food and a toast to the coming garden season and summer. I may not be able to paint the scene like the impressionist masters, but I can grow and cook the food, set the table, and find the right mix of people to make it happen.

# First Salad

The idea here it to combine a good mix of fresh garden greens, edible flowers, fresh herbs, and any fresh spring/early summer vegetables you like. The salad is then gently tossed (always using less dressing than you think you'll need) with either of the salad dressings. It's like eating summer in a bowl. Fresh, simple, the best kind of eating there is. Next time you're on a desert island . . .

*Serves 4*

> ½ pound assorted fresh seasonal greens, such as baby
>    spinach, lettuces, arugula, and baby beet greens
> ¼ cup fresh herbs, such as basil, chives, thyme, or lemon verbena,
>    left whole or shredded with your fingers into smaller pieces
> about 1 cup fresh spring vegetables, such as shaved baby fennel, freshly shelled
>    peas, tiny bits of lightly steamed asparagus, and fava beans
> ½ to 1 cup edible flowers, such as organically grown, non-sprayed nasturtium,
>    calendula, bee balm, chive flowers, and pansy
> ½ to 1 cup dressing of choice, *(pages 87–88)*

Thoroughly wash the greens, herbs, and flowers under very gently running cold water. Drain and dry thoroughly.

Gently toss the greens, vegetables (if using), and the herbs in a salad bowl, scattering the flowers on top. Add a few tablespoons of dressing and gently toss, serving the remaining dressing on the side.

# Basic French-Style Vinaigrette

Keep the vinaigrette in a well-sealed jar or bottle and it will keep, refrigerated, for several days.

*Makes about ¾ cup*

> 1 tablespoon Dijon mustard
> sea salt and freshly ground black pepper
> 2 tablespoons minced chives, parsley, basil, or thyme, or a combination
> ⅓ cup red or white wine vinegar
> ⅔ cup good olive oil

In a bowl, mix together the mustard with the salt, pepper, and herbs. Add the vinegar and stir well to create a smooth vinaigrette. Slowly whisk in the oil with a fork or whisk until it emulsifies, or thickens. Taste for seasoning, adding more salt, pepper, herbs, vinegar, or oil as needed. There is no magic formula (well, generally, it's one part vinegar to two parts oil, but it really is a matter of taste). Place in a glass jar or covered container and refrigerate. The vinaigrette will keep for up to 4 days.

87

## Variations:
- Substitute lemon juice for vinegar.

- Smash a clove of garlic with a pinch of salt and mash until it is paste-like. Then add the mustard, vinegar, oil, etc., for a garlic-flavored vinaigrette.

- Add 1 to 2 tablespoons milk, cream, yogurt, or sour cream for a creamy vinaigrette.

- Add a teaspoon or two of soy sauce, chopped scallions, and freshly chopped ginger.

- Add a touch of lime juice and lime zest.

### Tip
*You can also use balsamic vinegar, but you'll need just a touch less. Also, this is the time to take out that really good olive oil you've been keeping for something special. There are few dishes where the flavor of the oil really shines as much as it does in a vinaigrette. Use a fragrant Spanish, French, Italian, Greek, or California extra virgin olive oil.*

# Green Green Goddess Dressing

This is an herb-rich, creamy dressing that is light and flavorful and adds a gorgeous green color and thick, creamy texture to almost any salad.

*Makes about 1 cup*

1½ tablespoons fresh basil, chopped
¼ cup fresh chives, chopped
3 scallions, ends trimmed, chopped
¼ cup parsley, chopped
½ cup thick, Greek-style yogurt
2 tablespoons lemon juice
2 tablespoons white wine vinegar
½ cup olive oil
sea salt and freshly ground black pepper

In the container of a blender or food processor, blend the basil, chives, scallions, and parsley. Add the yogurt, lemon juice, vinegar, oil, salt, and pepper. Blend until smooth. Taste for seasoning and add more salt, pepper, lemon, or oil as needed. Place in a glass jar or covered container and refrigerate. Will keep up to 3 days.

---

# First-Harvest Pea *and* Lettuce Soup

There is one "trick" to making this soup: After shelling the peas, save the pods to make the pea broth. They infuse the broth with absolute pea-ness. Blend the mixture up. A touch of cream? Sure, but you really don't need it. A few chives? Couldn't hurt. You can make the soup a day ahead of time and reheat it just before serving. The soup can be served hot or cold, and can also be frozen for up to 3 months.

*Serves 4 to 6*

### For the pea broth:

2 pounds shelling peas, also called English peas
6 cups water or vegetable or chicken broth
1 onion, chopped
6 peppercorns
salt

### For the soup:

1½ tablespoons olive oil
2 sweet Vidalia onions, chopped
salt and freshly ground black pepper
¼ cup chopped fresh chives
1 bunch tender lettuce, cored, well washed, and dried
heavy cream, optional

Shell the peas and be sure not to throw away the pea pods. Place the pods in a large pot and place the shelled peas in a small bowl and set aside. (Sure, go ahead, eat a few.)

In the large pot with the pea pods, add the water or broth, onion, peppercorns, and a hefty sprinkling of salt. Bring to a boil, reduce the heat to low, and simmer, slightly covered, for about 1 hour. The broth should be sweet and taste of peas. If the broth still tastes weak (it should be subtly flavored), you can uncover it and let it simmer another 10 to 15 minutes.

In another large pot, heat the oil over low heat. Add the onions, salt, and pepper and cook, stirring occasionally, for 15 minutes or until the onions are soft and a pale golden color. Add the reserved peas and half the chives and cook, stirring, for 5 minutes.

Strain the broth over the peas and onions (gently pressing down to extract all the flavor and juices) and raise the heat to high. Bring to a boil, reduce the heat, and let cook, uncovered, for 15 minutes. Taste the broth — if it tastes weak, cook another 10 minutes. Add the lettuce and cook 5 minutes. Remove from the heat and let cool about 5 minutes. Working with a blender or food processor, puree the soup. Return to the pot and cook over moderate heat for about 10 minutes, or until slightly thickened and flavorful. Season to taste.

Serve hot with a sprinkling of the remaining chives and a drizzle of cream, if desired.

89

---

### ⇒ Other Ideas for Fresh Garden Peas ⇐

• Add them raw to hot linguine or your favorite pasta shape — so the heat of the pasta just begins to "cook" them — along with sautéed onions or leeks, a touch of cream or crème fraîche, and some fresh herbs.

• Make a fresh pea hummus by blending fresh peas and cooked chick peas with yogurt, ground cumin, fresh cilantro, mint, salt, and pepper. Serve on crackers, with raw vegetables, or as a spread for sandwiches and crostini.

• Make a pea salad using raw peas or lightly steamed peas mixed with chopped fresh mint, olive oil, and lemon juice.

• Make a pea pesto: puree raw peas with olive oil, a clove of garlic, salt, pepper, and toasted pine nuts and serve on top of or alongside grilled fish (particularly salmon and shrimp) or chicken.

# Ginger Shortcakes *with* Local Strawberries *and* Lemon Cream

I love the combination of ginger, lemon, and strawberries so I thought I'd make a ginger-scented shortcake and fill it with marinated local strawberries and a lemon-scented whipped cream. The recipe for this shortcake is very loosely based on one from James Peterson's *Baking*.

*Makes 8 shortcakes; serves 8*

### *For the ginger shortcakes:*

2 cups flour
1/3 cup sugar, plus 2 tablespoons for the glaze
1 teaspoon baking soda
1/2 teaspoon salt
1/2 teaspoon ground ginger, plus 1/8 teaspoon for the glaze
1 stick butter, chilled and cut into 8 pieces
1 egg
3/4 cup buttermilk, well shaken, plus 2 tablespoons for the glaze

### *For the strawberries:*

1 quart ripe local strawberries, hulls removed and cut in half if they are large
2 tablespoons sugar
1 to 2 tablespoons very thinly sliced crystallized ginger, optional

### *For the lemon whipped cream:*

1 cup heavy cream
2 tablespoons sugar
1 teaspoon grated lemon zest
1 to 2 tablespoons very thinly sliced crystallized ginger, optional garnish

Preheat the oven to 375 degrees.

To make the shortcakes, sift together the flour, 1/3 cup sugar, baking soda, salt, and 1/2 teaspoon of the ginger in a large bowl. Add the butter and using your hands, or a pastry cutter, lightly incorporate the butter into the flour mixture until the butter resembles coarse cornmeal.

In a small bowl, whisk the egg with the buttermilk. Pour the buttermilk mixture on top of the flour mixture and stir well to incorporate.

Flour a work surface and place the dough on top. Very gently knead the dough and form it into a flattened-out mound. Using your hands or a rolling pin, roll out the dough so it's 3/4-inch thick — you don't want it any thinner or the shortcakes won't have enough thickness and will cook too quickly. Use a 3-inch glass or biscuit cutter to cut out eight shortcakes. Place the shortcakes on a cookie sheet with a silicon mat or a piece of parchment paper.

Place the remaining 2 tablespoons of buttermilk in a small bowl and place the remaining 2 tablespoons of sugar mixed with the 1/8 teaspoon of ginger in another small bowl and set aside.

Bake on the middle shelf for 10 minutes. Remove and lightly brush the top of each shortcake with the buttermilk and sprinkle with the sugar mixture. Bake another 10 to 14 minutes, or until the shortcakes turn a pale golden brown and the edges are just starting to turn brown. Remove and cool.

Meanwhile, place the strawberries in a bowl and sprinkle with the 2 tablespoons of sugar and the crystallized ginger, if using. Let sit for at least an hour or until serving.

Whip the cream until soft peaks form. Add the sugar and lemon zest and whip until the cream holds its shape.

To serve, use a serrated knife to cut the shortcakes in half horizontally. Place an eighth of the strawberry mixture on the bottom half of the shortcake and top with a generous dollop of cream. Top with the other half; repeat with the remaining shortcakes, berries, and cream. You can garnish the plate with thin slices of crystallized ginger if you like.

## ⋙ Grilling Time ⋘

When I was growing up, grilling was man's work. Women may have cooked all the meals Monday through Saturday, but come summertime and Sunday it was the men who donned silly aprons and went outdoors and lit charcoal with all kinds of toxic lighter fluids. My dad, who didn't really know his way around the kitchen, was a master at grilling steaks, chicken, burgers, and hot dogs. This was suburban life, a la the 1960s, at its finest.

Grilling has come a long way. For many years I let my husband do all the grilling (Why? We were a liberated couple living in a new century!), but then I realized that getting outside on a spring or summer evening was a real treat. Out there, waiting for the grill to preheat, I would smell the herbs and the flowers, watch the stars emerge, and wonder how it was that women got relegated to a hot kitchen while men got to hang outside and have all the fun?

These days I grill year-round, keeping my barbecue just a few steps from the back kitchen door and easily accessible throughout the winter. I have been known to put on snow boots, a down jacket, and thick gloves and grill ribs or a leg of lamb in a raging blizzard. Hey, why not? I have experimented with just about everything on the grill—from vegetables and cheese to meats, poultry, and seafood, to fruits. There's not much that doesn't taste good (or better) cooked over an open flame.

There are, however, some tricks to successful grilling. Here are a few of my favorites:

- Always preheat your grill. Never place food on a cold grill or the timing will be off and your food won't obtain the requisite sear and brown grilling marks.
- If you've used a marinade on meats, fish, or poultry, be sure to remove it before grilling. Foods should not be dripping with oils or marinades when they hit the fire or they will flare up and burn. The only exception is dry rubs (mixtures of dry spices and herbs), which are meant to stay on food while it grills.
- The best way to gauge the heat of your grill is to have a built-in thermometer. If your grill doesn't have one (and most older models don't), you can simply place your hand a few inches above the grill grate. If it feels super-hot, like you're going to really get burned, it's hot, around 400 degrees. If you can keep your hand there for 4 seconds or more without feeling the heat, the grill is medium-hot. And if you can keep your hand there for more than 6 seconds it's low.
- When grilling food, don't keep flipping, poking, or prodding it. Leave the food alone on the grill and follow the cooking times—every time you flip or poke food it can lose juices and will take longer to cook and runs the risk of drying out.
- Get outside, smell the smoke, check out the stars, and enjoy the grilling experience year-round!

# Grilled Pork Chops *with* Grilled Rhubarb

We had an abundance of rhubarb and I wondered: Why doesn't anyone grill rhubarb? I decided it was time to try. I cut the stalks into chunks, sprinkled them with sugar to "marinate," and then grilled them and served them as a kind of sweet and sour topping for grilled pork chops. The result? Why didn't I think of this sooner?

Let the pork sit in the brine for at least an hour and up to 24 hours. It may seem like a fussy step, but brining produces really tender, moist pork. Serve with the Grilled Rhubarb *(page 95)*.

*Serves 4*

> 8 cups water
> 2 teaspoons salt
> 8 peppercorns
> 1 cinnamon stick, cut into pieces
> 4 allspice or cloves
> 2 bay leaves
> 4 center-cut or rib-cut pork chops, about 2 to 3 pounds, 1½ inches thick

Place the water in a large bowl. Add the salt, peppercorns, cinnamon stick pieces, allspice, and bay leaves, and stir to mix. Add the pork chops and cover and refrigerate for an hour and up to 24 hours.

Heat the grill to about 350 degrees or moderate heat. Once you preheat the grill and it seems hot, place your hand a few inches above the grill grate; it should feel quite hot, but not burning. Remove the pork from the brine and discard the brine. Pat the meat dry.

Place the chops on direct heat, cover the grill, and cook about 10 minutes per side, or until the internal temperature is around 140 degrees for rare or 150 degrees for well-done. Let the pork sit for 5 minutes before serving to let the juices settle. Spoon the grilled rhubarb on top and serve hot.

## Grilled Pizza *with* Grilled Zucchini, Tomato, *and* Pesto

If you use store-bought dough (or get it from your local pizza parlor, or even make your own), this is a really simple, satisfying way to make pizza. You can top the pizza with anything you like: pitted olives, tomato slices, anchovies, sausage, grilled eggplant slices, crumbled feta, thin slices of fresh mozzarella . . .

*Serves 4*

> 2 medium zucchini, thinly sliced lengthwise into long strips
> 2 1/2 tablespoons olive oil
> 1 onion, cut into eight sections
> salt and freshly ground pepper
> flour
> 1 pound pizza dough
> 1/4 cup pesto
> 2 medium tomatoes, thinly sliced
> 1 cup grated Parmesan cheese

Set up the grill for indirect grilling: preheat half the grill to hot, about 400 degrees, and make sure the other half has no direct heat under it.

Lightly brush the zucchini slices with 1/2 tablespoon of the oil. Grill over the hot part of the grill for about 2 minutes on each side, or until just soft and light brown. Add the onions and cook about 2 minutes on each side, then season with salt and pepper. Remove from the grill and set aside.

Working on a well-floured surface, roll out the dough to an oblong shape, about 16 inches long and 8 inches wide. Place the pizza dough on a cookie sheet and rub one side of the dough with 1/2 tablespoon of oil. Place all the ingredients on a tray and bring them all out to the grill.

Place the dough, oil side down, on the hot part of the grill for 2 to 3 minutes or until slightly puffed and just beginning to brown. Using tongs or a pizza paddle, gently flip the dough over. Brush the other side of the dough with 1/2 tablespoon of oil, and grill the other side over direct heat for 2 minutes. Carefully flip the dough over to the unheated side of the grill and carefully brush the pesto onto the dough and top with the zucchini and onion slices, the tomatoes, and finally sprinkle on the cheese. Season with salt and pepper. Cover the grill and cook for 10 to 12 minutes, checking the pizza occasionally and making sure it's not burning. You may need to rotate the pizza so one side doesn't cook more quickly than the other. The pizza is ready when the dough is slightly puffed, doesn't feel raw when touched, and the cheese is melted and the vegetables are warm.

### Tip

*This pizza is cooked using the indirect grilling method. Half the grill is heated until hot, leaving the other half without direct heat, giving you two cooking surfaces to work with so you can control the texture of your pizza and let it cook without burning. If using a gas grill, heat one side, leaving the other side turned off. If using a charcoal grill, heat the briquettes and then pile them all to one side, leaving the other side without heat.*

# Grilled Rhubarb

Serve with grilled pork chops *(page 93)* or other grilled meats or fish. Or serve the hot grilled rhubarb with yogurt or ice cream for a grilled dessert.

9 5

> 2 cups fresh rhubarb, ends trimmed, cut into 2-inch pieces
> 1/4 cup sugar, plus 1 tablespoon

Place the rhubarb in a bowl and sprinkle on the sugar.

Let "marinate" for about an hour at room temperature, or covered and refrigerated for up 12 hours.

Place a grill rack or basket on a hot grill, about 350 degrees. Place the rhubarb on the rack or basket and grill 5 minutes. Flip over and grill another 3 to 5 minutes or until the rhubarb is softened but not falling apart. Sprinkle with another tablespoon of sugar and serve.

# July

# BEST PIE:
# SUMMER RENTAL HOUSE COOKING

W e rented a house on an island with spectacular water views and a green stretch of lawn. It's a funky place, with rusty fixtures and sandy floors, beds that creak, and towels that have seen better days. But it's all about the water and its proximity.

As soon as we arrived, I rushed to the kitchen. My heart sank. This was not what I had in mind. I took stock of the drawers and cabinets. The knives looked like they hadn't been sharpened in more than a decade; the vegetable peelers and cheese graters were equally dull. There was no food processor or even a rolling pin, but I did discover a heavy, well-worn black cast-iron skillet. The cooking utensils — from the very thin wooden spoons to the cracked pie plate — all struck me as inferior. I had no interest in eating at overpriced, mediocre island restaurants. I had come to cook.

Later that day we headed to the fish market — a tiny gray shingled shack that smelled clean and salty, like an ocean breeze. The back door opened out onto the dock where old fishing vessels lined up to unload the day's catch. I felt like a bride-to-be at Tiffany's looking at diamonds. Everything was so fresh and locally caught (right off the boat took on new meaning) that it was hard to choose. We decided on the island sole, which was nowhere as sexy as lobster or swordfish or even local striped bass, but because the sole literally looked like it sparkled.

That night I pulled out the old cast-iron skillet and melted some butter and oil over high heat. I blanketed the filets in seasoned flour, very lightly, and sautéed them for just a few minutes on each side. They turned a perfect golden brown and, at the last minute, I threw paper-thin slices of whole lemon and tiny piquant capers into the skillet for an instant sauce. It was the freshest-tasting fish I'd eaten in years (except for a fish I once caught myself). I grilled a thick just-harpooned swordfish steak the next night (topped with pitted black and green olives and scallions and lemon juice) and roasted the striped bass with a thin coating of sharp mustard the night after that.

I learned to use the kitchen, with all it deficiencies, the way one might learn to play an old instrument. I compensated for the erratic heat the small gas stove gave off by pre-lighting it a few minutes before I was ready to cook so I'd be sure it was nice and hot. The freezer turned everything to a rock, so I learned to take the ice cream out 30 minutes before dessert.

Our island meals came from the fish store and the local farm, where we found everything from tender lettuces to juicy tomatoes, baby potatoes, peas, pattypan squash, and zucchini the size of thick pencils. Everything tasted enhanced, like really fresh food with a little something more. We spent long hours discussing the reasons: the freshness of island-raised food, being relaxed and on vacation leading to heightened sensations, and the sheer luxury of having a whole day spill out around the "job" of cooking meals. Perhaps it was the superior chef? I joked.

I figured the real magic might just be coming from the ill-equipped kitchen, that funky little room without a rolling pin, a blender, or any of the other fancy trappings that cooks these days think they need to make food taste good. My kitchen at home is filled with all the latest equipment. Garlic peelers, marble and wood rolling pins, a professional food mixer, a professional Cuisinart. You name it, I've got it. But on the island I was not relying on fancy tricks or equipment that supposedly make the job easier. I was simply focused on the ingredients and the joy of cooking with them.

Several days later, I attempted my first island pie. The tiny, wild island blueberries ripened the week we arrived. Each morning we mixed them into yogurt and granola and then, as the day moved on, popped them into our mouths when we craved something refreshing and slightly sweet and tart. But there were grumblings about a pie, so I set out to work.

At home I make pie crust in a food processor because I find the texture is more reliable when the dough doesn't spend a lot of time interacting with my warmer-than-normal hands. But in this kitchen I had to improvise. I found a cracked ceramic bowl and mixed the flour and butter, crumbling it quickly with my hands, being careful not to let it get too warm and soft. I added a tiny bit of ice cold water using my hands and not a spoon. I was getting into primitive cooking. The dough held together nicely so I shaped it into a ball, wrapped it up in foil, and placed it in the refrigerator for a few hours.

Next I poured the berries, small, tart, a brilliant blue-black into yet another cracked bowl. I thinly sliced one ripe peach and added it to the berries, hoping the sweetness of the peach juices would balance out the tartness of the blueberries. Then I added just a sprinkling of sugar, because I don't like fruit pies that taste of sugar and not fruit. I figure a fruit pie should be just about as sweet or tart as the fruit that goes into it. And, at the last minute, I threw in a teaspoon of lemon zest and vanilla extract because I love the way lemon, vanilla, and blueberries get along.

The absence of a rolling pin presented the biggest challenge. Eventually I found the fattest, cleanest bottle of red wine we had in the house and coated it generously with flour. I had to move the flour and sugar canisters off the kitchen's only table in order to roll out the chilled dough. The texture looked perfect; I could tell it would be a good crust with enough left over for a lattice topping.

I found the glass pie plate and realized the crack wasn't really a crack, but two sides of a pie plate precariously held together by nothing more than humidity. The only other option was an aluminum throwaway plate, and I felt discouraged again for the first time in days. A wine bottle would fill in for a rolling pin. And hands (even overheated ones) would substitute nicely for a food processor. But I refused to make my pie in a dollar throwaway aluminum pan. I rooted around in a few more cabinets and, just when I was about to give up, I discovered an old tin pie plate with tiny perforations at the bottom. I lined the plate with my crust and spooned a generous amount of the fruit in the center. I worried that the fruit would drip through the crust and then drip through the tiny holes at the bottom of the pie plate, but decided to take the risk. I knew the holes were there so the bottom crust would crisp up nicely and not get soggy from the fruit. I rolled out the scraps of leftover dough and laid a lattice topping on the pie, weaving the soft pastry strips in and out, and placed the pie in the freezer for a few minutes while the oven preheated. The smaller-than-normal fridge was filled with our food for the week, so the freezer was the only available space. I know pie crusts like to be chilled before they go into the oven, so I was hoping the freezer would work out okay so long as I didn't let it freeze.

The oven was preheated to 375 degrees. I quickly realized that there was no way this oven would be anything close to accurate, so I placed my hand in the middle to see if it felt hot, like 375 degrees should feel. I decided it was close enough and placed the pie on the middle shelf, hoping the five or so minutes the pie spent in the freezer chilled the butter in the crust enough, but not too much. There was no timer so I took a look at the clock on the kitchen wall and headed to the little beach just minutes from the house.

While I was swimming I imagined the fruit beginning to soften and bubble and the crust filling the whole empty house with its buttery essence. I swam a few minutes longer, conscious that I needed to be back in 45 minutes to check the pie, but the water was so luscious that I kept going. I lost myself in the swim — the whole point of a swim. Just one more circle around the buoy, I told myself. But as I headed back in I swam a little harder, a little faster, suddenly nervous about the pie.

When I got to the house I could smell the pie before I opened the screen door. I opened the oven door (of course, if there ever was an interior light it no longer worked) and the pie looked perfect. The fruit was bubbling, the crust was the pale golden color of a well-worn wedding ring, and the smell told me I had made it back just in time.

I gently removed the pie from the oven. I thought about food processors and sharp knives and rolling pins and marble countertops and my well-equipped kitchen back home. Later as we sat around the table, lit by cheap, dripping white candles, I thought this might have been the best pie I'd ever made.

# Fillet of Sole *with* Slivered Almonds, Capers, *and* Whole Lemon Slices

This dish should be taught in Fish Cookery 101 for its utter simplicity and surprisingly complex flavors. This recipe is like a fish piccata — fillets of sole or flounder are dredged in flour, sautéed over a high heat, and cooked until just tender. The pan is then deglazed with slivered almonds, capers, paper-thin lemon slices, and a splash of white wine or vermouth. Serve with pasta, rice, or potatoes.

*Serves 2 to 4*

> 1 cup flour
> salt and freshly ground black pepper
> 1 pound fillet of sole, flounder, or yellowtail flounder
> 2 tablespoons butter
> 1 tablespoon olive oil
> $1/2$ cup slivered almonds
> 4 tablespoons capers, drained
> 3 tablespoons lemon juice
> 1 lemon or Meyer lemon, preferably organic, washed, dried, and cut
>     into paper-thin slices
> $1/3$ cup dry white wine or dry white vermouth
> $1/4$ cup finely chopped fresh parsley

Preheat the oven to 275 degrees.

Place the flour on a plate or in a plastic bag and season with the salt and pepper.

Lightly dredge the fish fillets in the seasoned flour.

In a large skillet, heat half of the butter and oil over high heat and let it get nice and hot. Add a few fillets of fish, being careful not to crowd the skillet, and cook for 3 to 4 minutes. Gently flip the fish over and cook for another 2 to 3 minutes, or until the fish is just cooked through and golden brown. Place the fish on a warm serving plate, cover loosely with aluminum foil, and keep warm in the oven. Repeat with the remaining fish, adding butter and oil to the pan as needed.

When all the fish is on the serving plate, add 1 tablespoon of butter to the skillet. Reduce the heat to medium, add the almonds, and cook, stirring frequently, for 2 minutes. Add the capers, lemon juice, lemon slices, and wine, and cook for 2 to 3 minutes, or until the wine has been reduced by about half. Pour the hot sauce over the fish, garnish with the chopped parsley, and serve immediately.

### Tip

*Organic lemons are preferable in this dish because the entire lemon, rind and all, can be eaten.*

# Grilled Swordfish *with* Olive-Lemon-Scallion Topping

Swordfish has become a controversial fish in recent years. But when it's harpooned and fresh from the icy cold New England water, it's considered very good, safe eating. Here it's grilled and topped with briny olives, lemon juice, and crunchy scallions. This recipe will also work with any thick cut of fish, like halibut, tuna, or salmon.

*Serves 4*

### For the swordfish:

1½ pounds swordfish, tuna, or any firm seafood steak
2 tablespoons finely chopped fresh basil, or thyme
1 tablespoon olive oil
1 clove garlic, minced
1 teaspoon grated lemon zest
coarsely ground black pepper
1 lemon, cut into wedges

### For the olive-lemon-scallion topping:

½ cup pitted black olives, coarsely chopped
½ cup pitted green olives, coarsely chopped
¼ cup olive oil
2 scallions, finely chopped, white and green parts
1 teaspoon grated lemon zest
coarsely ground black pepper

Place the fish in a non-reactive pan or bowl and top with the herbs, oil, garlic, lemon zest, and pepper. Marinate for at least 1 hour and up to 4 hours, covered and refrigerated.

To make the topping, mix together the olives, oil, scallions, lemon zest, and pepper in a small bowl, and set aside. Cover and refrigerate if making ahead; don't make more than 4 hours ahead of time.

Preheat the grill for high direct heat, about 425 degrees. Place a clean grill rack on the grill and let it get hot for 3 minutes.

Remove the fish from the marinade, reserving the liquid. Place the swordfish on the grill, cover, and cook for 4 minutes. Gently flip the fish over, baste with any extra marinade from the bowl, cover, and cook another 4 to 5 minutes, depending on the thickness of the fish, or until just tender when lightly tested with a small sharp knife; it should yield and not feel "tough." Remove from the grill and place on a serving plate or platter. Spoon the olive topping along the middle of the fish, letting the excess drip down onto the sides. Serve hot with the lemon wedges.

# Berry Cobbler

This recipe came from my sister-in-law Andrea Gunst and, like the origin of so many recipes, she wasn't sure where she got it — a friend? an old *Gourmet* magazine? Here is my adaptation of the recipe — it works really well with wild Maine blueberries, raspberries, blackberries, strawberries, or any combination of stone fruit. What I love most about this dish is that it's made in three simple steps and can be served for breakfast or dessert topped with yogurt, whipped cream, or ice cream.

*Serves 4 to 6*

> 5 tablespoons unsalted butter
> 1 cup flour
> ³/₄ cup sugar
> 2 teaspoons baking powder
> ¹/₂ teaspoon salt
> ¹/₂ teaspoon cinnamon
> ¹/₂ teaspoon ground ginger
> ¹/₂ teaspoon ground nutmeg
> ²/₃ cup milk
> 2 cups berries

Preheat the oven to 375 degrees.

In an 8-inch gratin dish, shallow casserole, ovenproof skillet, or pie plate, melt the butter over low heat.

In a large bowl, mix the flour, sugar, baking power, salt, cinnamon, ginger, and nutmeg. Add the milk and whisk the batter lightly.

Place the berries on top of the melted butter and pour the batter on top of the fruit. Place on the middle shelf and bake 35 to 45 minutes, or until the batter is golden brown and the fruit is bubbling. Serve warm or at room temperature.

# Best Blueberry Pie

You don't need any fancy tools to make the best pie of your life. Simply plan on letting the crust chill for at least an hour before rolling it out. And once the pie is assembled, it should chill for at least 30 minutes before baking.

*Serves 6 to 8*

### For the crust:

2 1/2 cups flour
1/4 cup sugar
1/2 teaspoon salt
1 cup (2 sticks) unsalted butter, chilled and cut into small pieces
3 to 6 tablespoons ice cold water

### For the fruit filling:

4 cups wild or cultivated blueberries, raspberries, blackberries,
    or a combination of all
1 ripe peach or nectarine, peeled, pitted, and cut into thin slices
1/3 to 1/2 cup sugar or Vanilla Sugar *(page 105)*
1 1/2 tablespoons flour
1 teaspoon grated lemon zest
1/4 teaspoon vanilla extract
1 egg, beaten, optional

To prepare the crust, mix the flour, sugar, and salt in a large bowl. Add the butter and, using a pastry cutter or your hands, break the butter up into the flour mixture until it resembles coarse breadcrumbs. Mix in 3 tablespoons of the water, adding more if needed, until the dough begins to come together and there is no excess flour in the bottom of the bowl. Add another tablespoon or two of water if needed. Divide the dough in half, mound them each into a round, flat disc, and wrap each in a large piece of plastic wrap. Chill for at least an hour, or up to 48 hours.

To prepare the filling, gently mix the blueberries, peach slices, sugar, flour, lemon zest, and vanilla in a bowl, until all the berries are well coated. The berries can macerate in the sugar for several hours; cover and refrigerate.

Sprinkle a clean work surface with flour. Remove one of the chilled dough circles and roll it out to a circle about 11 inches across. Place the circle into a 9-inch pie plate, allowing the edges to fall over the sides of the pie plate. Place the blueberry mixture inside the dough. Roll out the other piece of dough to a circle about 11 inches across. Using a pizza cutter or a small sharp knife, cut strips about 1/2-inch thick out of the dough. Place the strips on top of the fruit filling, creating a criss-cross lattice pattern. Trim off any excess crust and crimp the edges of the dough together, creating a decorative pattern. Place the pie in the refrigerator for at least 30 minutes and up to several hours.

Preheat the oven to 375 degrees. Place the pie on a cookie sheet and brush the pastry with the beaten egg, if desired. (It will make the crust shiny and golden.) Bake for 40 minutes. Reduce the heat to 325 and bake another 10 to 12 minutes, or until the crust is golden brown and the filling is bubbling. If the pie begins to brown too fast, cover loosely with a sheet of aluminum foil. Let the pie cool slightly before cutting. Serve with ice cream or whipped cream, if desired.

### Tip

*To make Vanilla Sugar: cut a vanilla bean down the center lengthwise. Place it in a sugar pot and let it "flavor" the sugar for 24 hours and up to several months. Vanilla sugar is delicious in all kinds of baked goods where vanilla extract would be used.*

---

### ⇒ Freezing Berries ⇐

*Berries can be frozen successfully if you follow this simple method. Pick fresh berries — go on, keep picking, you'll be glad in January. Place the stemmed berries on a cookie sheet. Place in the freezer, making sure the berries don't touch or clump up. Freeze for about 1 hour, or until almost frozen. Remove from the freezer, separate each berry, and then place them in a plastic bag or plastic container tightly sealed. The berries won't clump up into one big mass if you pre-freeze them before bagging.*

# IF IT'S JULY, IT MUST BE
# HOUSEGUEST TIME

We've had houseguests. Lots of them. It's summer in Maine, and summer is when all good people want to visit our state. The phone started ringing towards the end of winter. "We thought we might come up for a few days this summer, and we'd love to see you." Sounded like a great idea in late March/early April, when all the world was mud and rain and time felt slow and open. Now it's practically the middle of July, and I want to know where my summer went?

Don't get me wrong. I love these people who are willing to travel long distances — some from across the country — to see us. And our houseguests should win awards for pitching in. One friend spent hours picking blueberries and raspberries so we could have pies each night. Other friends have gotten dirty pulling weeds and harvesting vegetables from the garden every evening. They strip their beds and do the dinner dishes and wake up with smiles. They are constantly remarking on the beauty of our state. "Maine is so gorgeous it makes you want to stay a month," they say in all seriousness. I panic momentarily.

The truth is a day is different when you wake up knowing that there are new people in the house, wanting your good strong coffee and something delicious for breakfast. And lunch. And dinner.

We tend to have very independent-minded houseguests. They rent cars and bicycles and head out for hours at a time, leaving us to work and go about our day in a somewhat normal fashion. But when visiting a food writer they all expect at least one meal. "Don't bother with anything fancy," they tell me. They don't really mean it when they say, "don't bother." They all hope I am testing recipes for a new book, something preferably with lobster. Everyone wants lobster.

Breakfast is the most problematic of these meals for me. I don't wake up hungry or in the mood to entertain — or cook. My favorite "guest" breakfast is simple, but always seems to be a hit: bowls of local yogurt, fresh fruit and berries, nuts, honey, and granola. If you make the granola ahead of time (it will keep for well over a week in a tightly sealed jar or bag), you can throw together breakfast in about five minutes. All you need to serve with the granola is a good, strong pot of coffee.

For me the best part about having visitors (other than getting to catch up with old friends and family) is the way they open my eyes to where I live. As we drive or bike around town I begin to see things differently.

Last week a friend from New York visited, and we took a bike ride. We went on my normal loop, across the river and past some pristine farmland, along the road with the organic dairy farm and the waterfall. I was able to see it all as a first-timer. The old red barns tilted slightly towards the earth, the cows grazing on the exceptionally green grass, and the river, dotted with kayakers, the fields of black-eyed Susans and daisies, the farmland with its perfectly symmetrical rows of corn, potatoes, and squash. Sometimes I'll take the day off and go to the beach with these visitors (why does it take an out-of-town visitor to make this happen?) and stop for an ice cream cone on the way home. I look closely at this place I call "home."

# Granola

Play around with this recipe, adding other nuts, dried fruit, or grains, and make this your own personalized granola. The granola will keep for about ten days.

*Makes about 6 cups*

> **vegetable oil spray for the pans**
> **3 cups rolled oats**
> **1 cup coarsely chopped walnuts, pecans, almonds, or your favorite nut**
> **1/2 cup coarsely chopped dried apricots**
> **1/2 cup unsweetened coconut or toasted coconut**
> **1/2 cup raisins or currants**
> **1/4 cup roasted sunflower seeds**
> **1/4 cup sesame or flax seeds**
> **1/4 cup sun-dried cranberries or cherries or blueberries, optional**
> **1 1/2 teaspoons ground cinnamon**
> **1 teaspoon ground ginger**
> **1/2 cup canola oil**
> **1/2 to 3/4 cup maple syrup, or honey**

Preheat the oven to 300 degrees. Line one large or two small rimmed cookie sheets with parchment paper or aluminum foil and spray lightly with vegetable oil.

In a large bowl, mix the oats, nuts, apricots, coconut, raisins, sunflower seeds, sesame seeds, cranberries, cinnamon, and ginger, and stir well to combine thoroughly. Add the oil, maple syrup or honey, and mix well, making sure the liquids thoroughly coat the dry ingredients. (You can also add a bit of maple syrup and honey, and add more or less, depending on how sweet you like your granola.)

Divide the mixture between the two cookie sheets. Bake for 45 to 50 minutes, or until the mixture is golden brown and looks cooked through, stirring the mixture once and turning the cookie sheets once during the baking. Let cool in the pans for 10 minutes, and store in a tin or a tightly sealed plastic container with wax or parchment paper.

# Cold Cucumber Soup *with* **Mint, Dill,** *and* **Lemon**

On a steamy summer day this is ideal cooling food. The soup is whirled in a blender or food processor and can be made in less than fifteen minutes. Chill for several hours (or overnight) and serve with chopped cucumber, dill, mint, and a drizzle of lemon oil. Warm pita bread triangles make a nice accompaniment.

*Makes about 4 cups; serves 4 to 6*

> 1½ pounds cucumbers, peeled, seeded, and chopped
> ¼ cup fresh dill
> ¼ cup fresh mint
> 1 cup low-fat milk or buttermilk
> 1 cup sour cream or low-fat plain yogurt
> salt and freshly ground black pepper
> 1 dash hot pepper sauce
> 1 tablespoon lemon-flavored olive oil, plus more for garnishing drizzle,
>     or 1 tablespoon olive oil plus ½ teaspoon grated lemon zest, optional

## *For the garnish:*

> 1 cup cucumber (peeled, seeded, and finely chopped) mixed with 2 tablespoons
>     finely chopped dill, and 2 tablespoons finely chopped mint
> drizzle of lemon olive oil or olive oil mixed with a touch of grated
>     lemon zest, optional

In the container of a food processor or blender, add the cucumbers, dill, mint, milk, and sour cream or yogurt and process until blended, but not totally smooth. Add the salt, pepper, and hot pepper sauce to taste, and drizzle in the olive oil (and lemon zest) if using. Place in a bowl or jar and chill for several hours.

Serve ice cold sprinkled with the cucumber-mint-dill garnish mixture and a drizzle of oil.

### Tip

*To seed a cucumber, simply cut it in half lengthwise and use a spoon to scoop out the seeds in the middle.*

109

# August

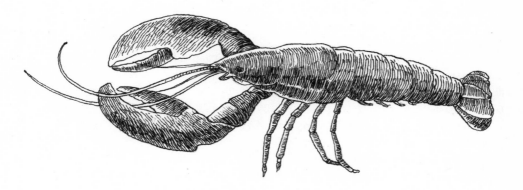

# LOBSTER WORLD, DEER ISLE, MAINE

**P**earl Hardy is wearing a navy blue T-shirt that says: "If a man speaks at sea where no woman can hear, is he still wrong?"

Hardy, a fourth-generation lobsterman, was born and raised in Deer Isle, a small island in Penobscot Bay, separated from the mainland by Eggemoggin Reach. Like so many of his fellow fishermen, Hardy has a good sense of humor and is a natural-born storyteller. It doesn't take much to get him talking. When I ask a question, any question, I am met with a thoughtful, ten- to fifteen-minute answer. Spending so many years at sea has given Hardy plenty of time to think about things. The weather. The lobster population. The politics that surround his profession. Lobster and its relationship to his island and his state.

We meet on the deck of a friend's house in the tiny village of Sunset, overlooking East Penobscot Bay. Seated on weathered Adirondack chairs facing the sea, Hardy welcomes a Bud Light. He has a salt-and-pepper beard, dark brown hair, thick eyebrows, and the rosy red complexion of a man who spends a great deal of time outdoors. The harbor is crowded with impressive-looking sailboats, but when a lobsterboat goes by, Hardy looks up from the conversation to register who's coming into port, and who's headed out. He appears to know everyone. Every so often he waves to people on a boat and they wave back. It's a small world up here.

Pearl Hardy has lived on Deer Isle all his life. He started lobstering when he was a boy, just nine years old. His father, also named Pearl, gave his son a small outboard and twenty-five traps, which he set out near Bear Island (a tiny dot of an island with a population of around twenty, just off Sunset). He pulled the traps by hand and got his first taste of the fishing life.

"Nine years old? Isn't that young?" I ask. But Hardy laughs. "Nope. That was just normal for us living out here. It's a lot more normal than I'm sure it sounds."

In his early fifties, Pearl Hardy has been in the lobster business pretty much ever since. For a short time, just after graduating from high school, he thought he might like to try something different. He got a job at the local grocery store, but it didn't take him long to realize that punching in every morning wasn't the life he was after. When asked what he likes best about fishing, Hardy doesn't hesitate. "Being self-employed. Getting up at three in the morning, getting ready to go. I put in a good day, work hard, but I'm usually home by two or three in the afternoon. And if I want to take tomorrow off, or fish until dark, I can do that.

"The thing about fishing is, we are in charge. And, there's no such thing as a typical day. Every day on the water is different. There's days that are absolutely gorgeous, flat calm, and then there's days where the fog's so thick you can't see a thing. A lobsterman I know was once asked what he liked best about his job. He said 'My office has three windows and the view is constantly changing.' That's pretty special, I'd say."

Pearl is married to Diane (his boat is the *Lady Diane*) and their son, Jason, now in his late twenties, is fishing as well. When I ask what it means to have his son, the fifth generation in the business, Hardy shrugs like it's not a big deal. "Yea, I'm glad Jason is fishing. He does well. He's got his own boat, and I'm very supportive." Hardy may sound nonchalant, but you can tell he is deeply proud of his son.

As much as things have changed in the lobster industry, they have also stayed the same. Deer Isle, with a year-round population of around 2,400, has a good summer tourism industry. Island towns are populated with art galleries, bakeries, and boutiques. The local quarry still produces the famous pink and grey speckled Deer Isle granite. But this is a place defined by lobster. According to Hardy, more than half of the kids raised on the island end up living here as adults and, in one way or another, their livelihood comes from lobster.

The lobster business is an insular world, one ruled by island families. Everyone we meet in the business seems to be third, fourth, or fifth generation. Could someone just move here, buy a boat, and set up business? Hardy laughs. "Well, it wouldn't be easy going." And then he says something that sounds like the lyrics to an old New England folk song: "If you're planning on coming here to start work as a lobsterman, hope you don't bring too much money cause you're gonna lose it, and hope you don't bring too many clothes cause you won't be staying too long."

But the last few decades have allowed a certain type of newcomer into the industry — the inclusion of women. One of Maine's more famous fisherwomen is Linda Greenlaw, author of several books about fishing. "We're seeing more and more girls on the boats all the time," explains Hardy. "A lot of girls are sternmen now; there's even a few girls who are captains with their own boats." What do you think about that? I ask. "Well, if she's good looking, she's fine with me. I mean you gotta look them over."

He laughs and takes a sip of beer. "No, no, seriously, I think it's perfectly fine. If a person can do the job, I don't think it matters. I think the girls want to go into lobstering same reason everyone does: the money. If a girl wants a job on the island, she can make about a hundred dollars a week, but on a boat she can make about $150 a day."

We spend a few hours talking lobsters. There are stories about his grandfather, his hard-working wife, memorable storms that have hit the island, and day-to-day fishing life. At some point the conversation turns to the difference between hard shell lobsters (fully grown with a hardened shell) and soft shells (or shedders), and Hardy's eyes light up.

"I once had the good fortune to actually watch a lobster shed," he begins. Other than scientists who study the molting behavior of lobsters in laboratories, not many people witness this phenomenon, which generally happens at the bottom of the ocean floor under rocks or mud. But here's what happened: when Hardy was "quite young," he accidentally pulled up a lobster while it was starting to shed, as the back shell was coming off. "I set it on the bulkhead of the boat to watch it do its thing. What I didn't realize at the time was that I should have put it in a bucket of water and watch it cause it was out of its natural ability to do what it normally does. I'm sure it was a harder scenario for that lobster to shed sitting on a bulkhead.

"When a lobster is shedding, they hide because they are so vulnerable. They find their spot, under a rock or in the mud, and shed the back shell. It just kind of splits right open and comes off. Then this lobster will kind of just lay there, and then all of a sudden it gets some energy and will flip its tail and the meat will start to come out of the tail shell. And then it stops and then after a few minutes it does it again. Tssssh, tssssh, tssssh," he says, mimicking the sound a lobster makes as it flips during the shedding process. "Then the tail shell will end up coming off. The claws are the last to work their way out. It's kind of odd and hard to understand, but a good-size claw, when he sheds, all comes out through the little knuckle, right where it attaches to the lobster. It just happens."

When a lobster sheds and has no shell, it's called a "jelly" and can't be sold. It takes a few weeks for a new shell to form. Shedders tend to be a few dollars less than hard shells per pound, making them a great bargain. Hardy thinks the meat in a soft shell is "way sweeter and more tender. It's one of the best-kept secrets. Truth is hard-shell lobsters can be tough."

And then we drift into more controversial territory. Over the past few decades, government regulations of the lobster industry have increased in an attempt to maintain the lobster population.

"The regulations are a very serious thing," Hardy says, suddenly getting quite stern. "When I started fishing years ago, a fisherman could do what he wanted. If a guy wanted to bust ass and work really hard and set two thousand traps and fish seven days a week, he could do it. Regulations are taking some of that away. There was talk recently about cutting lobstering out for five years down south of the Cape [Cod]. I tell you what that makes me feel: very scared cause if it happens down there it's gonna move up here one day. That's the thing that's very discouraging about regulations — it's not just what they're coming up with today, it's that they're gonna come up with something else tomorrow. When they told us we could only have an eight hundred-trap limit per boat, many fellas were against it, not so much because eight hundred traps was not enough, but they said if they do eight hundred today they're gonna bring it down to six hundred and then four hundred soon."

Is the fear of over-fishing real? "Absolutely not" says Hardy. "We farm our lobster; we are feeding them. We're throwing away a lot more than we're bringing in. We bait our traps with food [herring] to bring them in. Any given trap could have ten, fifteen, twenty lobsters in it, but you can't keep them all. You can't keep the oversized ones, or the undersized ones, or lobsters that have been seeded [this refers to female lobsters that carry eggs] . . . I mean, if you're bringing in [and keeping] one hundred lobsters and you're throwing back three hundred lobsters, you know, just do the math." ·

Fishing is an uncertain business and Pearl Hardy is acutely aware of this fact. We talk about the BP oil spill and its devastating effect on the shrimp industry in the Gulf. "Before the BP oil spill, I never thought something like this would happen," Hardy says, shaking his head. "Now that it has occurred, I think it's an eye opener for everyone. I think if something happens somewhere it can happen anywhere."

When I push Hardy a bit more on his fear of government regulations, he tells me I should meet Steve Robbins III, who runs the Stonington Lobster Co-op on the island.

Early the next morning Robbins agrees to talk. It's a hot, sunny, clear Saturday in August and Robbins pulls a few clean, empty lobster traps up onto the dock and arranges them like living room furniture for us to sit on. We're surrounded by squawking sea gulls, the busy harbor, and an occasional seal that pops its head out of the cold water. Robbins, in his early forties, a fifth-generation lobsterman, wears jeans, aviator-style sunglasses, and hiking boots. He is thin, tanned, and serious. After a series of surgeries and physical problems, Robbins gave up lobstering and became the manager of the co-op, a consortium of more than one hundred local fishermen, each of whom owns shares and has voting rights.

Robbins explains the situation this way: "Traditional lobstering is leave early in the morning, you go to work, you get home relatively late, and then you go and do it all over again. What I would like to see is more people realize that if they don't advocate for themselves by being more conscious and pro-active, there will be a point where they'll be negatively affected. They will lose their ability to do business and their freedom over time."

I think of Pearl Hardy and his love of the freelance fishing life. His ability to call the shots, name his hours. I think of the thousands of other lobstermen and women who have been fishing in the waters around this island, following their own rhythms for so many generations.

"Don't get me wrong," says Robbins. "Most fishermen are very hard working. But they are highly resistant to change — good, bad, or otherwise. They don't see that they have the power they actually do. If you had one hundred guys show up at a public hearing, or up at the State House, or the Maine Department of Marine Resources office and those one hundred guys said, 'I want this!' that would roll so many heads."

Despite all this, Robbins is optimistic about the future of lobstering. "Business is good. There's been plenty of lobsters this year and they started early. Every dollar generated by the landing of a lobster on this island means that money goes round and round and round. Everyone benefits — from the grocery store, hardware, fishing supply, bank, school, and the babysitter."

We are here talking politics, but I also want to know about lobster, so I ask him if he has a favorite way to eat it. I am ready for a simple recipe or two, but instead I get a crazy unpredictable story.

"Well here's a good one for ya. A friend of mine I used to go fishing with, well, he was drunk since birth 95 percent of the time. He was a very messy cook, but really good cooks, they usually have some sort of substance-abuse problem, just like Picasso. All the good ones suffer for their art. So this guy picked out raw lobster tails and he made a homemade mac and cheese, and we took the raw lobster tails and laid them out over the mac and cheese and baked it. That was the best thing I ever had in my entire life.

"Now prior to that we had not eaten in, like, three days, so you could have eaten a glove and it would have tasted good."

Later that afternoon I catch up with Pearl Hardy as he pulls into the dock of the Stonington Lobster Co-op. Together with his sternman, Travis Root, he's back from a morning of fishing. "We did well this morning, fine day. Shifted a lot of gear and brought in a good number of hard shells as well as some soft shells. We brought in around four hundred pounds." As he unloads the lobsters, as well as a big crate of rock crabs, he jokes with the guys on the dock. When they see me asking questions, one of them calls out to Hardy, "You telling her all kinds of B.S. as usual?" Everyone laughs and keeps loading lobsters onto the scales, and then into crates, where they will sit in the cold Penobscot Bay waters until they are shipped out to wholesalers a few hours later.

"We're all set," Hardy calls out as he fires up the *Lady Diane*. Just before he leaves the dock, I ask him if he's headed home for a lobster feast? "You know, I hate to say it, but I like lobster fine, but for me a big treat is a cold beer and a pizza."

And with that, he waves and heads off to the boatyard where he'll moor the *Lady Diane* for the night. Tomorrow he'll get up at the crack of dawn, pick up his sternman, head out to sea, and the whole cycle begins again.

## ⇛ A Few Lobster Stories ⇚

As so much of this country, and our culinary identity, becomes homogenized, Maine has managed to hold on to many of its food traditions. No matter where I travel in the world, I am constantly reminded of the deep connection between my home state and Homarus americanus, or Maine lobster. I can recall many scenes, in many cities and countries, that prove how central lobster is as an identifying symbol of Maine.

◆ Sitting in a restaurant in Beijing, when the waitress, wanting to try out her limited English, engages us in conversation. "Where you come from?" she asks.

"We live in Maine, in the northeastern part of the United States."

"Aah, Mean. I know Mean." And then she begins to move her fingers into pincers and pretends to attack me. "That is where the...how you say?

How you say it? From the o-shean? You know, the red fish? Where the labster lives. Yes, yes, you call it the labster?"

◆ Waiting for a streetcar in New Orleans, an older woman smiles at me, and we talk. We discuss the recent oil spill and the threat to local food sources. I tell her I live in Maine. "We got crayfish and shrimp," she tells me, "but soon all we gonna have left is them lobster from your freezing-cold state."

◆ A young mother buying produce next to me in a marketplace in Barcelona. "Oh, we have been to your state," she tells me. "So beautiful. The cold, the salt air, and all those delicious lobsters."

◆ Or the young hipster waiting in line next to me for the bathroom in Vancouver, Canada. "You live in Maine? Oh my God, do you, like, eat lobster, like, every single day?"

117

# Lobster Roll

A classic Maine lobster roll contains fresh lobster meat mixed with mayonnaise and, sometimes, finely chopped celery. That's it. The salad is stuffed into a buttered and grilled hot dog roll. You can do it the old-time Mainer way, but I happen to my like my version better, combining freshly cooked lobster meat with just a touch of mayonnaise spiked with lemon juice, lemon zest, chives, and scallions. And I like serving it on pieces of buttered, grilled baguette because I love the crunch and texture of French bread with the tender lobster meat. But a buttered hot dog roll isn't bad, either.

*Serves 2 generously*

> two (1-pound) lobsters, or 1 cup cooked lobster meat
> 1½ to 2 tablespoons mayonnaise
> 1½ teaspoons fresh lemon juice
> ½ teaspoon grated lemon zest
> 1 tablespoon minced fresh chives
> 1 tablespoon very finely chopped scallion
> salt and freshly ground black pepper
> 1 tablespoon unsalted butter
> two (3-inch) pieces of baguette or crispy bread, or two hot dog rolls

Fill a large pot with 2 to 3 inches water and bring to a rolling boil over high heat. Add the lobster, shell side down, cover, and cook for about 11 minutes, or until a leg pulls out of the body easily. Remove from the boiling water, drain off any water, and let cool.

Separate the tail from the body. Using a fork, remove the tail meat. Crack the claws and remove the meat. Enjoy the bodies (see "What a Body!" *page 125*). Cut the tail in half lengthwise and remove the thin black vein. *Coarsely chop* the tail and claw meat and set aside.

In a bowl, mix the mayonnaise (use more or less, depending on how creamy you like it), lemon juice, zest, chives, scallion, just a touch of salt, and pepper to taste. Fold in the lobster meat. You can make the lobster salad several hours ahead of time, but not more than 3 to 4 hours ahead. Cover and refrigerate.

In a skillet, melt the butter over low heat. Cut the baguette pieces in half lengthwise and brown the inside of the bread in the melted butter until it just begins to turn golden brown. Alternately, melt the butter and brown the hot dog rolls until they begin to turn a golden brown, flipping them over so they get toasted and buttery on both sides. Divide the lobster mixture between the bread or the rolls.

## Variations:

- 1 tablespoon drained capers
- 2 tablespoons finely chopped celery
- lime juice and zest instead of lemon
- buttery, tender lettuce leaves
- slices of ripe tomato
- 2 strips of cooked country-style bacon, thin slices of buttery avocado, or very thin slices of red onion

---

### ≫ Lobster Tips and Trivia ≪

- *Always remove the rubber bands from lobster claws before you cook them or you'll have rubbery-tasting lobster. Be careful once you remove the rubber bands because the lobster is very much alive and will snap at your fingers if you're not careful.*

- *How do you tell the difference between a male and a female lobster? Look between its legs, of course. If you look between the legs of a female lobster you'll find the two feelers, or swimmerets, located at the base of the tail. If they're hard, it's a male; if they're soft and flexible, you've got yourself a lady. Some think females are sweeter; others swear by the males.*

- *Males grow larger claws, have narrower tails, and spikes on the underside of the tail. Females have broader tails and feathery hairs on their swimmerets.*

- *The red roe, or coral, found in female lobsters, is considered by many to be a delicacy.*

- *A 1½ pound lobster yields about 1 cup of meat.*

- *To relax a lobster before putting it in a pot of boiling water, flip the lobster over so the shell side is in the palm of your hand. Use your fingers to stroke the feelers, or swimmerets, located at the base of the tail. The lobster will go limp and calm down.*

- *Lobster is said to have fewer calories, less total fat, and less cholesterol than lean beef, poached eggs, and roasted, skinless chicken. It is high in vitamins, calcium, phosphorous, zinc, and iron. It is also high in omega-3 fatty acids, the "good cholesterol."*

# Lobster *and* Corn Chowder

In Maine, chowder can be found on menus everywhere — from diners and coffee shops, to the state's finest restaurants. It's the way a Maine chef can tell you what they're made of. This one is a winner. The lobsters are steamed and the water they are cooked in becomes the basis of a hugely flavorful broth. The corn adds a sweet August flavor that brings out the very best in the lobster. Don't be scared off by the length of this recipe — it's basically three simple steps. The chowder only improves when it's made a day ahead of time.

*Serves 6 as a first course and 4 as a main course*

> salt
> three (1½-pound) lobsters
> 3 peppercorns
> 1 carrot, chopped
> 1 stalk celery, chopped
> 1 bay leaf
> 3 strips thick country-style bacon, optional or 1½ teaspoons olive oil
> 1 large onion, finely chopped
> 1 pound potatoes, peeled and cut into ½-inch cubes
> ¾ cup heavy cream
> 1 dash cayenne pepper
> freshly ground black pepper
> 4 to 5 ears corn, with the kernels shucked off, about 4 cups raw corn kernels

Place 8 cups of cold water into a large pot with a generous dash of salt and bring to a rolling boil over high heat. Place the lobsters in the water shell side down, cover, and cook for about 11 minutes, or until the lobsters are just about cooked; they will turn bright red and when you pull a leg it will come off, but not as easily as a fully cooked lobster. Remove the lobsters from the water and let cool; *do not throw out the cooking water.*

Remove all the meat from the lobster tail and claws. Cut the lobster meat into 1-inch pieces and set aside. Add all the shells and the bodies back to the pot and bring the water to a rolling simmer over moderately high heat. Add the peppercorns, carrot, celery, and bay leaf. Reduce the heat to moderate and let simmer for about 45 minutes, or until the broth is somewhat reduced (to about 7 cups) and flavorful. When you take a sip it should taste of lobster. Keep cooking if it tastes weak. Strain the broth and discard the shells; you can keep the lobster bodies for snacking if you like.

In a large pot, cook the bacon until crisp on both sides, about 8 minutes. Drain the bacon on paper towels, being sure to keep the bacon fat in the pot. Chop the bacon into small pieces and reserve. If you're not using bacon, heat the oil in a large pot over low heat.

Over low heat, add the onions to the bacon fat or oil. Cook, stirring, for 4 minutes. Add the potatoes and cook another 4 minutes, stirring. Strain 7 cups of the reserved lobster broth into the pot and bring to a boil. Reduce the heat to moderate and let simmer about 10 minutes, until the potatoes are just tender.

Add the cream and simmer for 5 minutes. Add a dash of the cayenne and pepper, and cook another minute. Add the reserved lobster meat and the corn and let heat through, another 5 to 7 minutes over low heat. Taste for seasoning, adding more salt, ground pepper, or cayenne as needed. Serve hot, topped with a sprinkling of the reserved bacon, if desired.

# Latin–Style Lobster Salad

As much as I'm a purist when it comes to eating lobster, this salad — flavored with fresh corn, lime, and avocado — is delicious and refreshing served as a summer lunch or light dinner. All the fresh flavors, colors, and textures work well with the lobster meat. Serve with warm biscuits, French bread, or tortillas. The salad can be made, covered, and refrigerated, several hours ahead of time.

*Serves 2 to 4*

> 1 cup cooked lobster meat, cut into small cubes
> 1 cup fresh raw corn kernels, shucked off the cob of 2 or 3 ears of corn
> 1/2 ripe (but not overly ripe) avocado, cubed
> juice of 1 large lime
> 1 tablespoon olive oil
> salt and freshly ground black pepper
> 1 dash hot pepper sauce
> tender butter lettuce leaves

In a medium-size bowl, gently mix the lobster, corn, avocado, lime juice, oil, salt, pepper, and a dash of hot pepper sauce; season to taste. Scoop the salad in the lettuce leaves and serve with any of the accompaniments listed above.

# Angry Lobster

This recipe came from an old friend, chef Neil Kleinberg. This is not for the weak of heart: a live lobster is chopped into bite-size pieces, tossed with olive oil, garlic, basil, rosemary, and crushed red pepper and roasted in a hot oven. This is a very unconventional way to prepare lobster, but once you try it you'll be hooked. Serve with pasta (tossed with olive oil and garlic or your favorite tomato sauce) and garlic bread to mop up all the excellent lobster-flavored juices from the bottom of the pan.

*Serves 4*

> four (1-pound) live lobsters
> coarse sea salt
> freshly ground black pepper
> 1/4 cup olive oil
> 8 large cloves garlic, very thinly sliced
> 1 cup fresh basil leaves, torn into large pieces
> 2 to 3 sprigs fresh rosemary, cut into 2-inch pieces (stem and herb)
> 1 teaspoon crushed red pepper flakes

Place the live lobster on a work surface shell side down. Using a large sharp knife, make an incision where the tail and body connect, with the blade facing the head of the lobster. Push down the knife, cutting the body into two pieces. (This will kill the lobsters instantly.) Using your hands, twist the tail off and pull off the claws, removing the rubber bands. Separate the body into halves, then cut into quarters, slicing across the body. Remove and discard the stomach sac at the top of the head. Remove the tomalley and set aside.

Cut the tail into four pieces. Separate the knuckles from the claws. With a quick action, use the back of the knife to crack the top of the claw. Turn the knife over and cut the claw in half at the joint. Make a small incision in the soft bottom part of the knuckle and cut in half. At the end of the process you should have 16 pieces of lobster. Repeat with the remaining lobsters.

Place the lobster pieces in a large bowl and season with salt and pepper.

Preheat the oven to 450 degrees. Place a large shallow roasting pan in the hot oven and preheat for 5 to 10 minutes, or until very hot.

Remove the preheated pan from the oven and carefully add the oil to the pan. (Careful, it may splatter.) Place the lobster pieces in the hot pan, shell side down, and roast for 6 minutes, or until the shells turn red. Sprinkle the garlic on the bottom of the pan (you want it to brown) and then sprinkle the top of the lobsters with the basil, rosemary, and crushed red pepper. Roast another 6 to 8 minutes, or until the lobster is cooked through but still tender; it will continue to cook once it's removed from the oven. Test the tail by placing a small sharp knife into the tail meat; it should feel firm but not rubbery. Remove from the oven and serve hot.

---

### ⫸ Cooking Tips ⫷

• *Steaming produces the juiciest, most tender meat. Fill a large pot with 2 to 3 inches of water. (Adding salt or a few strips of fresh seaweed is controversial. Lobsterman Pearl Hardy says that you don't need to add salt to the water. He says, "Lobster are plenty salty all on their own.") Bring the water to a rolling boil and add the lobsters to the pot shell side down so all the juices get caught in the shell and are not lost in the pot. Cover and let steam 11 to 12 minutes for a 1-pound lobster and about 20 minutes for a 2-pounder. To test for doneness, simply pull off one of the legs; if it pulls off easily, the lobster is ready. Drain and serve with melted butter, lemon wedges, and plenty of oversized paper napkins. A baked potato, a few ears of corn on the cobs, and an ice-cold beer or two wouldn't hurt!*

• *Always make sure the water is at a full rolling boil at high heat before placing a live lobster into the water. You want to add them to the pot, cover it immediately, and get the water back up to a boil as fast as possible. Do not keep peeking under the lid to check on the lobster; you will reduce the water temperature and throw off the cooking time.*

♦ *When cutting up lobster for a salad or to use in another preparation, be sure to cut the tail down the middle lengthwise and remove the thin black vein, like you do with shrimp.*

# Grilled Lobster *with* Garlic-Lemon-Herb Butter

If you've never grilled lobster outdoors, you're in for a treat. This lobster is cooked over indirect heat — meaning the coals are pushed off to one side (or a gas grill is only heated on one side), allowing the lobster to cook slowly and become moist, slightly smoky, and infused with garlic, herbs, and butter. If you are squeamish about the idea of cutting a live lobster, ask your fish store to do it for you, but be sure to cook the lobsters within an hour after they have been cut. Your best bet for this recipe is using a soft-shell lobster. Since the shell is soft, it's easier to cut the lobster down the middle. And because of the soft shell, the heat of the grill cooks the lobster meat more evenly and quickly. If you're working with hard-shell lobsters, you may need to add another 2 to 3 minutes to the cooking time.

*Serves 4*

6 tablespoons unsalted butter, at room temperature
2 cloves garlic, minced
3 tablespoons chopped fresh chives
2 tablespoons chopped fresh thyme
1½ tablespoons chopped fresh basil
½ tablespoon chopped fresh tarragon
1½ tablespoons fresh lemon juice
a generous grinding black pepper
four (1½-pound) live lobsters, preferably soft shell
1 lemon, cut into wedges

Place the butter and garlic in a small saucepan and simmer over low heat for about 4 minutes, or until the butter is bubbling and the garlic has softened, but not browned. Remove from the heat and add the chives, thyme, basil, tarragon, lemon juice, and pepper and stir well to mix all the ingredients. The butter can be made several hours ahead of time; cover and refrigerate until ready to cook the lobsters.

Preheat the grill for indirect heat, pushing the hot coals off to one side and leaving the other side without direct heat. When working with a gas grill, simply heat *only one side* of the grill until hot, about 400 degrees. When you place your hand over the grill grates it should feel quite hot.

Meanwhile, prepare the lobsters. Place them on a clean work surface, shell side down. One at a time, place a tea towel over the lobster's head and plunge a knife into the body directly below the head and split the lobster open, cutting it down the middle, almost all the way through. The two halves of the lobster should still be attached and not completely separated into two halves. (This technique may seem gruesome, but many experts claim it's more humane than plunging the poor things into boiling water.) Remove and discard the stomach sac at the top of the head. Alternately, have your fish store cut the lobster for you, but be ready to cook the lobsters within an hour or so.

Divide the herb butter between the lobsters, placing it in the body and throughout the tail of each, pushing the butter into the meat.

Place a grill rack on the side of the grill *without* the direct heat, and place the lobster on it shell side down, so that you don't lose any juices. Cover the grill and cook for about 15 minutes. Remove the cover and cook for another 2 to 6 minutes, depending on the size of your lobsters, until the tail meat feels just firm, and not soft and raw. The tomalley or liver should not be a dark green but a paler more cooked-looking green. Remove from the hot grill, place on a platter, and scatter with the lemon wedges.

---

### ➤ What a Body! ➤

*Lobster bodies are the undiscovered secret of the lobster world. Most people throw them away, discarding all kinds of delicious meat and juice. Lobster and fish stores throughout Maine and New England often sell the cooked lobster bodies for a ridiculously low price, like four bodies for a dollar! I mean you can barely buy a pack of gum for a dollar!*

*So how do you eat a lobster body? Pull the body out of the shell. Rip off the lobster legs and....well the best way to put it is this: chew, suck, slurp. Stick the whole leg in your mouth and bite down and...chew, suck, slurp. Rip the body apart and chew and separate the meat attached to the legs. There is much delicious meat and juice to be had. Don't worry about getting dirty — that's what those ridiculous lobster bibs are all about. This is dirty business, so dig in. Chew, suck, slurp. Got it?*

# Lobster *and* Mango Salad

The sweet, juicy flavor of fresh ripe mango complements sweet lobster meat perfectly. Serve on a bed of mixed greens or with taco chips like a lobster and mango salsa. This salad should not be made more than an hour ahead of time.

*Serves 2 to 4*

> 1 ripe mango
> 1 cup cooked lobster meat, cut into small cubes, from a 1½ pound lobster
> 1 tablespoon fresh cilantro or parsley, finely chopped
> juice of 1 lime
> 1½ teaspoons finely chopped fresh ginger
> 1 small fresh yellow or red tomato, chopped
> salt
> hot pepper sauce, to taste

To cut the mango, hold the mango upright on a cutting board and, using a large sharp knife, cut just over ⅓ of the fruit off the side of the mango. Repeat with the opposite side so you have two large pieces of mango, without the irregularly shaped pit. Use a small sharp knife to cut a tic-tac-toe pattern into the fruit, with lines about ½ inch apart. Push the mango skin to make the tic-tac-toe cubes pop out into little squares. Cut the squares off, away from the peel. Repeat with the other side.

In a bowl, mix together the lobster, mango, cilantro, lime juice, ginger, and tomato. Season to taste with the salt and hot pepper sauce.

# September

# PRESERVING SUMMER

When we moved to Maine in the early 1980s and were looking to buy an old farmhouse, there always came a point in the house tour when the Realtor would say, "And, of course, you want to come downstairs and check out the plumbing and electrical situation." John always seemed interested in taking these excursions (after all, bad plumbing and faulty electrical wires could be a deal breaker). I know I *should* have cared more, but I didn't like the idea of schlepping down those steep, dusty, cob web-infested cellar stairs. As we headed into that netherworld of electrical boxes and mysterious critters, I was often way-laid by something far more interesting than plumbing fixtures.

In many eighteenth-century Maine farmhouses, small shelves were built into, or alongside, the cellar stairs. As I begrudgingly made my way "down cellar" (a new, slightly scary term for me), I stopped to examine the array of old Mason jars I inevitably discovered on those shelves. Lined up like ancient relics, the jars, often blue-tinted, were filled with peach wedges, corn- and pepper-studded relishes, blueberry and strawberry jams and jellies, and tomatoes floating in watery substances that reminded me of experiments leftover from a high school biology lab.

I would call out to John and the Realtor, "You go on ahead and check stuff out, I'll be down in a minute," but I rarely made it all the way down. Like an anthropologist, I would examine the canning jars and wonder at the lives that went on in these old farmhouses. I imagined the woman of the house, apron-clad, pots of boiling hot water, dozens of old jars lined up ready to be sealed. I could feel her exhaustion, the enduring heat of a September day when the entire garden was ready to be harvested and canning needed to happen before produce rotted. I could see the piles of ripe tomatoes and the endless ears of corn. The bowls filled with ripe berries. And I could practically hear the children calling out to their preoccupied mother, and her frustrated response. "Later, children! I must finish up the canning."

The Realtor would pass me on the way up the stairs. "Do you know much about the people who originally lived here?" I'd ask. "Who built this house? Who canned these tomatoes, these peaches, this relish?" I knew these weren't normal first-time-home-buyer-type questions, but those canned goods fascinated me. It seemed to me that, contained within those jars, were stories and secrets to be revealed, not to mention years of history.

We eventually bought one of those farmhouses. Our old Colonial dates to somewhere between 1760 and 1790. When we discovered the house we swooned over the old wooden beams and the gorgeous wide-planked floors. The fireplaces were all in working order and the windows seemed larger, brighter than most of the other eighteenth-century farmhouses we explored. But it was also the large garden and the canning jars on the cellar stairs that let me know we had found a home with a strong culinary history.

Much has changed since the eighteenth-century, when our farmhouse was built. Although gardening and putting food up is still a time-honored tradition for many Mainers, most of us don't *need* to can fruits and vegetables in order to eat well during the colder winter months. We have freezers and markets that ship food to us from all over the globe. We live in a world where strawberries and tomatoes are sold year-round, from far-away lands.

But tending a garden means that every September there will be dozens of tomatoes that ripen within a week or so of each other. It means the basil will be tall and lush at the end of the season, and the peppers, green beans, onions, leeks, garlic, and eggplants will all need to be harvested. The late-season raspberries and blackberries will ripen with sweet juice whether we have time to pick them or not. After all the weeding and watering and loving care, I am simply not willing to waste any of the food I grow.

129

It's mid-September and there are six of us clustered around the stove in my kitchen. One friend arrived with peaches from a local orchard and someone else has a huge bushel of peppers and plum tomatoes. We have eggplant, beans, and several varieties of heirloom tomatoes from my garden and pears from the old tree behind my barn that, for some reason after close to thirty years of lying dormant, has decided to bear gorgeous fruit.

I am not a fanatical canner, but I have figured out a way to get the canning done without breaking my back and spending long hours *alone* in the kitchen. I make a party of it, inviting friends to come with their produce and canning jars and lids and spend a day/night cooking and canning and putting up our home-grown fruits and vegetables.

We break up the tasks. You chop. I peel. You get the canning pots full of boiling water and sterilize the Mason jars. Someone else cranks the tunes. We may start out mellow (folk, jazz) but by the time the sun sets there will be some funk. We're going to need James Brown to keep us going. Canning for hours can be exhausting work, but when you're surrounded by friends, good food, and good music, the energy stays high.

The berries are easy — they go into sealed plastic bags and then into the freezer. Local peaches are spiced and often doused with brandy before they go in jars, or they are peeled and simmered into a thick ginger- and cinnamon-laced peach butter *(page*

135). Tomatoes are roasted and either canned or frozen *(page 131)* and the eggplant and peppers are chopped and simmered into a pungent caponata or relish. The cucumbers are brined for pickles and excess beans will be pickled or put into bags in the freezer. The garlic, leeks, and onions are piled into a tall basket and stored "down cellar."

We spend the whole day/night putting up relishes, jams, jellies, chutney, and sauces, sharing all the fruit and produce and dividing up the goods. The next morning, looking at the glass jars all lined up, I have a deep sense of satisfaction. It's a lot of hard work, there's no doubt about it, but it's also so much fun to hang out with friends who care about making the most of their garden produce. I am never sorry come February when I open a jar of roasted tomato sauce *(page 131)* to throw on some pasta, or open a bag of summer berries to make a pie *(pages 104–105)* or a cobbler *(page 103)*, or spread some peach butter *(page 135)* on my morning toast, and the taste, smells, and flavors of summer come alive.

And, of course, there's the sense of tradition in canning, of paying respect to all the women who lived in this house before me, and all the hard work they did to make this land (and this house) a wonderful place to live, garden, raise children, and, of course, cook.

# End-of-the-Season Roasted Tomato Sauce

Roasting at a high temperature gives tomatoes a rich, slightly smoky flavor, and onions and garlic become sweet as they caramelize. For those with a fear of canning, this is a no-fail tomato sauce that can be refrigerated for three to five days, or it can be frozen in a tightly sealed plastic bag for several months. The sauce can also be placed in sterilized Mason jars and processed for 30 to 35 minutes in a boiling water bath; it will keep for up to a year. Toss the sauce with pasta, serve it over grilled chicken or fish, or in any dish that calls for regular tomato sauce. Feel free to add pitted olives, drained capers, chopped sweet or hot peppers, anchovies, or any fresh herbs you have on hand.

*Makes 12 to 14 cups*

> 10 pounds ripe tomatoes, any variety, cored and quartered
> 8 medium onions, peeled and quartered or chopped
> 5 cloves garlic, peeled and left whole
> 5 cloves garlic, peeled and finely chopped
> 1½ cups chopped fresh herbs such as rosemary, basil, thyme, oregano, parsley, and/or chives
> ⅔ cup olive oil
> ½ teaspoon salt, or to taste
> a generous grinding of black pepper
> a few tablespoons sugar (optional)
> optional ingredients

Preheat the oven to 450 degrees.

In a large roasting pan, gently toss together the tomatoes, onions, whole and chopped garlic, herbs, olive oil, salt, and pepper. Roast for 25 minutes. Gently stir the vegetables. Roast for another 25 minutes and toss gently. Add any additional ingredients you'd like and roast for another 45 minutes to an hour, or until the tomatoes are softened and somewhat broken down into a sauce, with a golden brown crust on top. Remove and taste for seasoning. If the sauce tastes bitter, add a few tablespoons of the sugar.

Let cool and place in clean, sterile jars or tightly sealed plastic bags, and refrigerate, freeze, or can. If canning, process for 30 to 35 minutes.

### Tip

*I don't peel my tomatoes when I make this sauce because high-temperature roasting produces a peel that is very edible. However, if you truly dislike tomato peels, simply remove them by placing the tomatoes in a pot of boiling water for 60 seconds and then, immediately, place them into a bowl of ice cold water. The peel will come off easily.*

131

## ※ Top Canning Tips ※

These canning tips come from my fellow canner and dear friend Karen Frillmann, who lives and cans in Upstate New York.

1. **Decide what you want to eat** later in the winter and a make a big batch of it. Tomato sauce with mushrooms and puttanesca without anchovies is standard. Each year there are extras like brandied peaches, ketchup, pickled beets, raspberry jam, whole tomatoes, and applesauce.

2. **Start on something easy.** For several years friends would come and visit and we would pick gallons of local raspberries, come home, and make up jars of jam. They tasted great and it was not that difficult. Given as gifts, people were very impressed, and I loved the knowledge of knowing exactly what was in the jar I was giving away. That success made me feel more courageous about taking on more complicated food preserving.

3. **Can with like-minded people** who enjoy prepping food, working together, and focusing on a project through various steps. My current canning group has been going for twenty-one years and it's produced hundreds of preserved dinners.

4. **It's only worth canning very high-quality produce.** Ideally the food should come out of your own garden. And that's the way you really make this cost effective. Buying seconds from farmers or going to pick-your-own farms is very satisfying and allows you to capture the great flavor of freshly picked produce. "Seconds" are the bruised or not-quite-perfect-looking produce that are ideal for canning —

and generally about half the price of the regular produce. You can ask a farmer to put aside a box of seconds for you when they are harvesting.

**5. Sharpen your knives, gather your cutting boards, and pull out your large bowls for sorting ingredients.** Have large pots for sterilizing and processing your jars. Long-handled tongs are useful for pulling hot jars out of boiling water.

**6. There are many trusted books and online sources available devoted to canning.** This is a technical process, so do follow directions and be careful. We've never made anyone sick, but we have had canning seals fail and we are careful to check before we split up our jars. (Check the Resource section on page 194 for more information.)

**7. Make a comprehensive shopping list** — olive oil, vinegar, good salt, sugar — and check your spice rack. It's a pain to have to run off to the store multiple times for forgotten items.

**8. Run your used jars through a dishwasher or wash carefully** in the sink. You do this before you sterilize them in boiling water. We use the same jars from year to year and carefully check for chips in the glass. And then buy new lids each year.

**9. I start thinking about canning in early August** and start talking to farmers at my local farmer's market as well as local farms I frequent. The better the planning, the more relaxed we can all be when we sit down to the mounds of produce and begin the task of preserving community as well as great food.

133

---

### ⋙ **A Few More Practical Canning Tips** ⋘

• *Always add sauces and liquid to canning jars when they are warm and not boiling hot or cold. The only exception is when making pickles with salt or a cold brine.*

• *Always fill jars ¾ full and not all the way.*

• *If there are bubbles trapped within a jar, take a clean kitchen knife and run it around the rim of the jar. This will loosen any air bubbles.*

• *Be sure to run a paper towel or clean kitchen towel around the rim after you've filled the jars to make sure there's nothing spilling over. Even the smallest bit of sauce on the outside edge can cause bacteria to grow.*

• *After the jars have come out of the boiling water and are cooling you'll hear a "pop" sound, which indicates the vacuum seal was made, the jars are cooling, and the seal is tight.*

• *Once you remove the jars, don't tip them or dry off the water that may collect on top of the lid. You don't want anything to touch the seals before they cool and set. Once the jars are cool, make sure your seal is tight by checking the lid; it shouldn't be loose or come off when you tug gently at it.*

• *If you have a bad seal you have several options: place in a clean jar, reseal, and reprocess. Or place the sauce in a plastic bag and freeze or simply place the unsealed jar in the refrigerator and use within a few weeks.*

• *Store canned goods in a cool, dark spot.*

• *Collect old Mason jars at yard sales, flea markets, antique shops, etc. Cracked or chipped ones can be used as flower vases or pencil holders, but not for canning. New Mason jars are also good, but don't have quite as much character. Visit your local hardware or feed stores for new canning lids and seals.*

• *Make your own labels. Buy blank stick-on labels at an office supply shop and write out your own label in colored ink or a small drawing. Be sure to always add the date so you can keep track of the shelf life of your canned goods.*

# Spiced Peach Butter

This is like a cross between jam and fruit butter. Find a local peach farm and ask for seconds (the bruised, slightly imperfect fruit) and make up this sweet peach butter. Nutmeg, cinnamon, ginger, and allspice provide the spice and a touch of sugar adds some extra sweetness. The only other ingredient is patience—you want the butter to simmer slowly for about 2 to 3½ hours until the butter is thick and full of the fragrant sweetness of a perfectly ripe peach. You can place the butter into clean glass jars and refrigerate for up to 2 weeks or process it and keep for up to a year. It's excellent on morning toast, muffins, pancakes, waffles, or serve with a cheese platter or roasted meats. It also makes an excellent glaze on roast pork. Feel free to make this butter using nectarines as well, or a combination of stone fruit.

*Makes about 10 pints*

10 pounds ripe peaches
1½ cups sugar
1½ teaspoons ground cinnamon
1½ teaspoons ground ginger
½ teaspoon ground nutmeg
½ teaspoon ground allspice

Take the ripe peaches and, working over a large bowl to catch any juices that drip, use your fingers to peel the skin off the fruit. Discard the skin and pit and chop the peach flesh making sure to catch all the juices in the bowl. Place all the chopped peaches and juices in a large pot. Add the sugar, cinnamon, ginger, nutmeg, and allspice and bring to a boil over high heat. Reduce the heat to low and let simmer, uncovered, for about 2 to 3½ hours, stirring occasionally, depending on how much juice the fruit contains. Be careful to stir the bottom of the pot and make sure it doesn't burn. Taste for seasoning and add more sugar if you like and more spices if you want a spicier fruit butter. When the fruit has broken down and the juices have thickened enough to coat a spoon, remove from the heat and let cool a bit. (It will continue to thicken when it cools.)

The butter will keep in a covered jar in the refrigerator for several weeks. If canning, process the butter for 30 minutes.

# Slow-Simmered Tomato Sauce

You'll need a few hours to make this luscious sauce, but most of the time the sauce will be simmering while you're off doing something else. Use a good variety of garden tomatoes — I like to use at least three or four varieties, since some add sweetness and others are more acidic — to create a well-balanced sauce.

*Makes 12 to 14 cups*

> 3 tablespoons olive oil
> 2 cups finely chopped onions
> 4 cloves garlic, 2 finely chopped and 2 thinly sliced
> salt and freshly ground black pepper
> 10 pounds fresh garden tomatoes
> 1/2 cup finely chopped parsley
> 1/2 cup finely chopped basil
> a touch of sugar, as needed

Bring a large pot of water to boil. Fill a large bowl with ice water.

In another large pot, heat the oil over low heat. Add the onions, half the chopped and sliced garlic, salt, and pepper, and cook, occasionally stirring, for 15 minutes.

Meanwhile, place a few tomatoes at a time in the boiling water for about 1 minute. Remove with a slotted spoon and immediately place in the bowl of ice water. The shock of the hot and cold causes the peel to separate from the tomato. Remove from the ice water and, using your fingers, remove the peel from the tomato. Core and chop the tomatoes, and set aside. Repeat with the remaining tomatoes.

Add the chopped, peeled, and cored tomatoes to the onions, along with the remaining garlic, parsley, and basil. Let cook, uncovered, over low heat for about 2 hours, stirring occasionally. Taste for seasoning, adding more salt or pepper as needed. If the sauce tastes acidic, add a touch of sugar.

You should now have a thick, chunky sauce. Place in jars or freezer bags and refrigerate (for 3 to 5 days), or process the sauce in canning jars. If canning the jars, process for 30 to 35 minutes.

## Variations:

◆ There are so many flavors you can add to this sauce. Think of it as a basic tomato sauce and add any or all of the following, or keep it pure and simple:

◆ For a spicy puttanesca sauce, add: 1 cup drained capers, 6 anchovies, about 3 tablespoons anchovy oil, 1 1/2 cups finely chopped, pitted black olives, and a dash of red chile flakes to taste.

◆ For an olive-flavored sauce, add: another 2 tablespoons olive oil when the sauce is done and is off the heat, along with 2 or 3 cups pitted black and/or green olives, coarsely chopped.

◆ For an herb-flavored sauce, add: 1 cup of chopped fresh thyme, sage, oregano, chives, and/or rosemary during the last 10 minutes of cooking.

◆ For a super-garlicky sauce, add: 6 cloves garlic to the sauce instead of 4. Roast a whole head of garlic by placing it in a small ovenproof skillet in a 350 degree oven for about 15 minutes, or until the cloves feel soft when you press them with your fingers. Remove, let cool a bit, and then squeeze the roasted garlic cloves out of their skin and into the sauce during the last 30 minutes of cooking.

# Wild Maine Blueberry Syrup

This syrup can be used to make a natural blueberry soda or spritzer. A tablespoon or two is fabulous added to fruit salads, pie fillings, or mixed drinks (try mixing with vodka or rum and fresh mint leaves). The syrup will keep in the refrigerator in a tightly sealed jar for a week or two, or it can be frozen (place in empty ice cube trays or plastic bags or small plastic containers) for several months.

You can also use raspberries, blackberries, cultivated blueberries, or strawberries, as well, or a combination of all four.

*Makes 1¼ cups*

**1 cup water**
**½ cup sugar**
**2 cups fresh wild Maine blueberries**

Boil the water over high heat. Add the sugar, stir, and cook over high heat for 5 to 10 minutes, or until the water just begins to turn a pale caramel color. Reduce to moderate heat, add the berries, and cook 10 minutes. Cool off the heat for 5 minutes. Place the berries and liquid in a strainer set over a wide heat-proof bowl and strain the berries through, pushing down to extract all the liquid. Let cool.

### Tip

*Make a wild-blueberry mimosa by mixing 1 tablespoon blueberry syrup with
1 cup sparkling white wine or champagne.*

# SWEET SEPTEMBER CORN

The thing about not having access to something all the time is that it becomes precious — sometimes overly precious. Think about it. Long-distance love. Your child leaving home. An amazing meal you had in a far-away country. A great cheese available only in its native land.

For me, all these examples are pertinent. When it gets to be September, and I know the days are numbered before the fresh, sweet summer corn disappears, I tend to become obsessed. I eat it for breakfast, lunch, and dinner. For breakfast I make sweet fritters that we drizzle with maple syrup. For lunch there's corn on the cob (the purest form of corn bliss) sprinkled with a touch of sea salt. It's so rich and bursting with freshness around this time of year that butter seems redundant. And for dinner I sauté it and place a sauce on top of grilled fish, poultry, or throw it into an early fall soup or stew.

And then when I see the tall, majestic stalks beginning to dry out and dwindle in the fields, I get a panicky feeling, like someone is taking away my best friend. I grab several dozen ears and make corn relish for winter eating and have even been known to freeze the fresh kernels to use for winter soups and chowders. (It's always a disappointment because the texture changes so much when it's frozen.)

Bottom line: Corn is August/September food, and come late fall it's time to say goodbye. Some foods are just not meant to be eaten out of season.

# Herb *and* Feta Corn Fritters

A simple batter is made by mixing corn kernels with egg, flour, and milk and a handful of fresh garden herbs, crumbled feta cheese, and scallions. The savory fritters are served with a lemon-herb butter and are delicious served for breakfast, lunch, or dinner. You could also add a finely chopped sweet or spicy pepper to the batter. The fritters are delicious served on top of an arugula or spicy greens salad.

*Makes about ten small fritters; serves 3 or 4*

> ½ **cup flour**
> ½ **teaspoon baking powder**
> ¼ **cup milk, plus 1 tablespoon**
> **1 large egg, lightly beaten**
> **2 cups fresh corn kernels, cut off 2 to 3 cobs**
> **2 tablespoons finely chopped fresh herbs (basil, sage, rosemary, chives, oregano)**
> **2 tablespoons very thinly sliced scallions, white and green parts**
> ½ **cup** *finely crumbled* **feta cheese or goat cheese**
> **salt and freshly ground pepper**
> **3 tablespoons olive oil, canola oil, or grape seed oil, or a combination**

In a large bowl, sift the flour and baking powder. Add the milk and whisk until smooth. Beat in the egg and then gently mix in the corn, herbs, scallions, cheese, salt, and pepper.

In a large skillet, heat the oil over moderately high heat. Drop 2 to 3 tablespoons of batter into the hot oil and cook 2 to 3 minutes on each side, or until golden brown. Serve hot.

# Maple Breakfast Corn Fritters

This recipe makes a sweet fritter by adding maple syrup to the batter (and omitting the herbs and scallions) and serving the finished fritters with maple syrup. Either way, you want to use really fresh corn.

*Makes about ten small fritters; serves 3 or 4*

> $1/2$ cup flour
> 1 pinch salt
> $1/2$ teaspoon baking powder
> $1/4$ cup milk
> 1 large egg, slightly beaten
> 2 tablespoons maple syrup, plus syrup for serving
> 2 cups fresh corn kernels, cut off 2 to 3 cobs
> 3 tablespoons vegetable oil
> warm maple syrup, for serving

In a large bowl, sift the flour, salt, and baking powder. Add the milk and whisk until smooth. Beat in the egg and maple syrup and then gently mix in the corn.

In a large skillet, heat the oil over moderately high heat. Drop 2 to 3 tablespoons of batter into the hot oil and cook 2 to 3 minutes on each side, or until golden brown. Serve hot, with a small pitcher of maple syrup on the side.

# Fresh Corn-Cracked, Pepper-Scallion Cornbread

Sweet, fresh corn kernels and scallions are mixed in a buttermilk-based cornbread to create a moist, double corn-flavored bread. Serve warm or at room temperature with chowders, soups, or salads. You can also let the cornbread cool thoroughly, cut into wedges, and cut in half to use as the basis for a cheese sandwich, or a ham and spicy mustard and arugula sandwich. Serve with Ramp Butter *(page 68)* or Whipped Maple Butter *(page 47)*.

*Serves 8*

    2 cup cornmeal, stone-ground and organic, if possible
    1 cup flour
    1 tablespoon sugar
    1 tablespoon baking powder
    1 teaspoon baking soda
    $1/2$ teaspoon salt
    a generous amount of coarsely ground black pepper
    3 eggs
    2 cups buttermilk, well shaken
    3 tablespoons unsalted butter
    2 tablespoons olive or canola oil
    1 cup finely chopped scallions, white and green parts
    1 cup corn kernels, cut off 1 to 2 cobs

Preheat the oven to 400 degrees.

In a large bowl, whisk together the cornmeal, flour, sugar, baking powder, baking soda, half the salt, and the pepper. Make a well in the center of the bowl and add the eggs. Whisk in the eggs and then add the buttermilk. Whisk together everything until it is fully incorporated.

In a large ($10^{1/2}$-inch) cast-iron or heavy ovenproof skillet, heat the butter and oil over low heat. Add the scallions and corn, the remaining salt, and more cracked pepper and cook, stirring, for 3 minutes. Remove from the heat and pour into the batter. Gently fold in to incorporate. Pour the batter back into the cast-iron skillet.

Place the skillet on the middle shelf and bake for 25 minutes, or until a toothpick or cake tester inserted into the center comes out clean. Let cool a few minutes and serve in wedges, hot or at room temperature.

# Grilled Swordfish *with* Sautéed Corn, Tomato, *and* Basil

The combination of sweet corn, tomato, and basil makes a great topping for grilled swordfish (or any type of fish, meat, or poultry), but also works as a crostini topping (on slices of grilled crusty bread), or inside tacos or burritos.

*Serves 4*

### For the fish:

1½ pounds swordfish steak, about 1 inch thick (you could also use salmon, halibut, or tuna)
1½ tablespoons olive oil
a coarse grinding of black pepper
2 tablespoons fresh lemon juice
1 lemon, cut into wedges

### For the topping:

4 ears corn, shucked
2 tablespoons olive oil
1 to 2 cloves garlic, very thinly sliced
3 tablespoons very thinly sliced fresh basil
1 tablespoon fresh thyme, chopped
1 scallion, very thinly sliced, white and green parts
1 large tomato, chopped
salt and freshly ground black pepper

Preheat the grill (charcoal, wood, or gas) until hot, about 400 degrees. When you place your hand over the grill grates it should feel very hot. Place the swordfish in a small dish and coat on both sides with the oil and pepper. Place a clean grill rack on the grill and let it get hot. Place the swordfish on the grill, pour half the lemon juice on top, cover, and cook for 4 minutes. Gently flip the fish over, add the remaining lemon juice, cover, and cook for another 4 to 5 minutes, depending on the thickness of the fish, or until just tender when lightly tested with a fork.

Meanwhile, make the corn sauté: using a sharp knife, cut the kernels off the corn.

Heat the oil in a medium skillet over moderate heat. Add the garlic and cook, stirring, for 30 seconds. Add the corn kernels, half the basil, the thyme, and the scallions and cook for

2 minutes, stirring. Add the tomato, salt, and pepper and cook for another 3 to 5 minutes, or until the tomato just begins to soften and the corn is still crunchy but hot. Add the remaining basil and more salt and pepper if desired. (The mixture can be made several hours ahead of time and reheated just before serving.)

Place the swordfish on a platter and spoon the warm corn mixture down the middle of the fish, letting it spill onto the sides. Serve with the lemon wedges.

# Fresh Corn, Tomato, *and* Mint Salsa

The combination of sweet corn kernels mixed with yellow and red tomato, green pepper, a touch of jalapeno, and fresh mint is a good one. Serve this salsa with chips, or use it as a quick, simple topping for pan-fried or grilled fish, meats, or poultry. The salsa can be made about an hour or so before serving; cover and refrigerate until ready to serve.

*Makes about 4 cups*

143

> 1$\frac{1}{2}$ cups corn kernels, about 2 cobs
> 1 cup finely chopped sweet green pepper
> 1 yellow tomato, finely chopped, about $3/4$ cup
> 1 red tomato, finely chopped, about $3/4$ cup
> 1 large scallion, very finely chopped, white and green parts
> 3 tablespoons olive oil
> 1$\frac{1}{2}$ tablespoons red or white wine vinegar
> 2 tablespoons finely chopped fresh mint
> 1 teaspoon finely chopped fresh jalapeno with seeds, optional
>     (depending if you want salsa with a bite or not)
> salt and freshly ground black pepper

In a medium bowl, gently mix all the ingredients. Season to taste with the salt and pepper.

# October

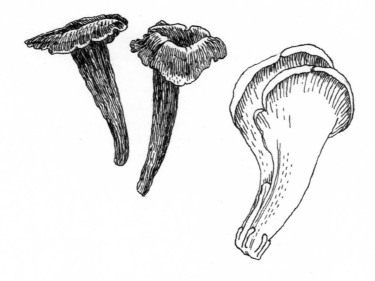

# THE MUSHROOM MAN

Rick Tibbets pulls up in front of Hugo's restaurant in downtown Portland in a four-wheel-drive Jeep that says "Fungi" on the plates. Tibbets is a professional forager, and one of his customers, Rob Evans, Hugo's chef and owner, has agreed to introduce me to Tibbetts for a day of mushroom hunting. We are heading to the mountains in search of wild matsutakes. October is prime time for matsutakes, and if we're lucky, Tibbets has hinted, we might also find chanterelles, black trumpets, honey mushrooms, and porcinis. "But, hey, no promises."

"Follow me," he instructs, starting up the Jeep. "I'll *try* to go slow." Evans revs up his BMW motorcycle, and I trail behind in my red Prius, good environmentalist that I try to be, desperate to keep up.

Driving out of Portland I watch the cityscape morph into gorgeous countryside. The leaves are insane, brightly lit like a backdrop for a movie starring New England. We head northwest, towards the White Mountains. It's the last weekend of the Fryeburg Fair, but Tibbets knows the back roads. He's a back-roads kind of guy. We drive down a bumpy dirt road (I worry the Prius is too low for the potholes, but it perseveres), across a wooden covered bridge that dates from 1866, across several rivers and streams. After close to two hours of driving, we arrive at a parking lot in the White Mountain National Forest.

Tibbets has asked that I not be more specific about the locale. He smiles, but it's the kind of smile that says "If I tell you where I pick my mushrooms, I'm gonna have to hurt you." I think about Tony Soprano.

Tibbets isn't a Mafia-looking or -acting kind of guy. He is mellow and soft spoken. He wears a thick sweatshirt with a camouflage pattern on it, dark pants, and hiking boots. He doesn't carry a basket or knapsack (where will the mushrooms go?). He looks like a younger, healthier Keith Richards — like a guy who likes to spend hours alone in the woods. I can tell he's not sure about me yet. (I spent close to a year trying to persuade him to take me out foraging and only when chef Evans agrees to come along for the ride — and the mushrooms — did he finally agree.)

We head into the woods and the warm October sun disappears; the sky goes dark and starts to spit cold rain. It's mid-October, but suddenly the air feels like December. We are in a gulley, near a bend in the stream, in what Tibbetts calls "a humidity vortex." Simply put, the air is thick, rich, and damp, perfect growing conditions for mushrooms.

Tibbetts has been studying mushrooms since he was fifteen. (After much prodding, he finally admits to being in his early fifties.) He reads every book and article he can get his hands on, but insists "books alone won't teach you enough about mushrooms." He also talks to academics, professors, and other mycologists (the word *mycology* comes from the Greek, meaning "fungus" and is the branch of biology that studies fungi) to constantly educate himself. But mostly he spends long hours walking alone in the woods, observing. "You gotta just get out there, open your eyes, and start hiking."

We hike for about twenty minutes, talking about mushrooms without a single sighting. "This could be a bust," Tibbetts tell us. Evans and I look crushed, like kids being told there might not be candy on Halloween. We keep walking, rain picking up, air getting colder as we climb. "Don't move," Tibbetts whispers, looking right at me. I'm sure there's a bear around or something equally terrifying. "You're standing on a honey mushroom. Don't crush it." Our first sighting is directly under my hiking boot, and I gently lift my foot to examine the three-inch mushroom. It is, as its name suggests, the color of honey — a buttery amber brown. Tibbetts picks it and explains that it's a really good eating mushroom. "Honey mushrooms are the world's largest fungus," he tells us. "They grow in huge areas generally at the base of tree trunks, usually oaks. They taste like straw mushrooms. But you want to get them when they're young and small."

"That's the thing about Rick," says Evans, who has been foraging with Tibbetts several times over the past five years. "He has an eye for these things. I was once standing in a field of honey mushrooms and didn't even see them. Rick's eye is so trained that he can spot a mushroom growing under a pile of leaves while we see nothing."

How does someone become a professional forager in the twenty-first century? "Well, you gotta like food," says Tibbetts. "I was a chef before I became a forager. I grew up around Polish and German folks who picked vegetables. I thought it was fun. So I started studying mushrooms."

You may be thinking what I was thinking as Tibbetts talked. How can anyone earn a living foraging wild food? The pickings are richer than you might imagine. Tibbetts starts the year in late April and early May looking for fiddleheads *(page 71)* and ramps, or wild leeks *(page 64)*.

"Then come the pheasant-back mushrooms, followed by prized morels, and oyster mushrooms. June is slow except for the stinging nettles, but come July the black trumpets, chanterelles, and yellow-feet chanterelles appear. As we head to the end of summer the cepes and porcini appear — two prized mushrooms that chefs are always looking for (and are willing to pay top buck for). Come fall the chicken and hen of the woods, and the white matsutakes sprout. And the season winds down toward late October," says Tibbets.

On this cold, windy, October day the pickings appear to be slim. Just when we are about to give up, we hike up a narrow ravine and Tibbetts points to a cluster of white matsutakes. He picks them close to the ground, stem and all. There's a cluster of about a dozen mushrooms, but Tibbetts only takes three or four.

He talks intensely about the importance of leaving mushrooms behind. "There are these guys that come into the woods with rakes," Tibbetts says with an undisguised tone of disgust. "But when you rake the ground you expose the mycelium (the interwoven, branched, threadlike filaments that make up most mushrooms) and you get bacteria, and raking makes the mycelium sick. They won't continue to grow. It's a fisherman mentality. *Take all you want now.*" Tibbetts is, of course, referring to the idea that if you clean out the ocean — dragging nets and picking up all sorts of living sea life — you won't be left with anything for the next generation. The same holds true for mushroom foraging.

We are wet and tired, but happy. Rob starts talking about how he likes to cook the matsutakes — slicing them really thin, sautéing them in olive oil and garlic, and then adding a dusting of good Parmesan. "They taste like pasta," he tells me. If Rob Evans, a James Beard–award winning chef, tells me that matsutakes can taste like pasta, I guess I should believe him, but I'm dubious. Later that night when I do exactly as he describes, I could swear I'm eating tender, earthy-flavored fresh fettuccine with garlic, oil, and cheese. Who knew?

Evans sums it up this way: "Eating food that Rick brings me from the forest is my favorite part of the season. When he brings me mushrooms and wild vegetables it's more organic than organic, more regional than regional, more seasonal than seasonal. These foods have been growing here in the woods since before any of us can even imagine."

After a few hours in the woods we have a few bags (turns out Tibbetts had several plastic supermarket bags tucked into his back jean pockets) filled with golden chanterelles, honey mushrooms, white matsutakes, and several oyster mushrooms. Back in the parking lot we find a huge granite slab and lay out the mushrooms according to type — the matsutakes in a cluster next to the honey mushrooms, etc. I am reminded of Halloween and the ritual my daughters had every year coming home from trick or treating and laying out the "goods" according to candy type — M&Ms next to the Almond Joys next to the Snickers. My excitement over finding these mushrooms is about on par with my young daughters and their adoration of candy. I am positively gleeful. Tibbetts smiles at me as I count the mushrooms aloud. I think I might have finally won him over.

*A Note of Caution: Picking wild mushrooms can be dangerous. Only go out mushroom foraging with a trained guide or someone who really knows their stuff.*

# Sautéed Matsutake "Pasta" *with* Parmesan Cheese

You can try this recipe with any type of wild mushroom, but if you slice fresh matsutakes thinly, sauté them with good olive oil and garlic, and then serve them with a dusting of Parmigiano Reggiano, you will swear you're eating fresh pasta. Serve with warm, crusty bread.

The idea for this recipe came from chef Rob Evans of Hugo's in Portland.

*Serves 2*

> 8 matsutake or porcini, or fresh wild mushrooms
> 2 tablespoons olive oil
> 2 cloves garlic, finely chopped
> 1 tablespoon chopped fresh rosemary, optional
> sea salt and freshly ground black pepper
> 1/3 cup grated Parmesan cheese

Clean the mushrooms with a damp paper towel to remove any dirt and debris. Cut off about 1/2 inch from the bottom of the stem, and then thinly slice the mushrooms and the remaining stems.

In a large skillet, heat the oil over high heat. Add the garlic and cook for 10 seconds. Add the mushrooms, rosemary (if you like), salt, and pepper, and cook 2 to 3 minutes on each side, or until golden brown and beginning to soften.

Remove from the skillet and sprinkle with the Parmesan. Season to taste and serve immediately.

149

# Roasted Wild-Mushroom Soup

Use portabellas or shiitakes, cepes, or any wild mushrooms you can find for this earthy, creamy soup.

*Serves 4 to 6*

> 1 pound fresh portabella mushrooms
> 2 teaspoons olive oil
> 3 medium onions, peeled and chopped
> 3 cloves garlic, peeled and chopped
> salt and freshly ground black pepper
> 1 teaspoon chopped fresh thyme
> 1 tablespoon chopped fresh rosemary
> 2 tablespoons dry sherry or red wine
> 5 cups vegetable, chicken, or beef stock
> a touch heavy cream, crème fraîche, or yogurt, optional

Preheat the oven to 400 degrees.

Gently clean the mushrooms using a moist paper towel. Cut the bottom 1/2 inch off the stems and then cut the mushrooms into chunks.

Grease the bottom of a medium to large roasting pan or ovenproof skillet with 1 teaspoon of the oil. Add the mushrooms, onions, garlic, salt, pepper, thyme, rosemary, and remaining oil and stir well.

Roast on the middle oven shelf for 20 to 25 minutes, stirring once or twice, or until the vegetables are tender. Remove the roasting pan from the oven and pour the sherry into the pan, scraping up any bits clinging to the bottom of the pan. Add the stock. Let cool a minute or two.

Transfer the soup to a blender or food processor and, working in batches, puree the mushroom mixture and all the juices, blending until smooth, but taking care when blending hot liquids.

Transfer to a medium-large pot and season to taste. Reheat and add a touch of cream, crème fraîche, or plain yogurt, if desired. The soup really doesn't need much! Serve hot with crusty bread.

# AN APPLE EXPEDITION

I t was the kind of early October weekend that makes New England famous. Warm, intense sun, cool breezes, and a sky so blue and clear it doesn't look quite real. The leaves were beginning to turn, and seeing one or two branches blazing with maroon and orange paints a pretty picture. One of my favorite orchards was open for picking, offering the last of the summer peaches and ten types of apples, so we packed into the car and drove north.

The fields surrounding the farm had all been hayed and those wonderful cylindrical rolls were left to dry on the parched earth. There had been no rain for more than two weeks.

The fruit farm is nearly empty in the early afternoon and we march up to the counter like excited children. Just the idea of picking fresh fruit off a tree gives me a thrill. But when the young woman at the counter tells us the last of the peach trees have been picked clean just an hour before, my heart falls. My friend has come to visit from New York, and I promised her a peach-picking expedition. The young woman tells us we can walk through the orchard and try our luck. I'm feeling optimistic. We manage to fill a very small bag with the last of the peaches, but it's only enough for a pie or two. There are still some hearty 'Harrow Beautie's and several tenacious Madisons. But to breathe in just a little of that sweet nectar, and pick some of those fuzzy, ripe orange peaches makes the trip worth it.

As we're leaving the peach orchard we see all kinds of excitement under the apple trees. A family of four pulls a bright red wagon overflowing with apples. The kids munch away, sweet juice dripping down their chins. It's hard to remember that when apples are fresh off the tree they have that kind of juice. The little girl's white dress, adorned with hand-embroidered roses, had a zigzag line running down the middle from apple juice stains. She looks happy. Damn the dress.

We stroll through rows of apple trees, reading the names of the different varieties out loud like stanzas from a poem: "Mutsu, Empire, Jonagold, Ginger Gold, Northern Spy, Idared, Cortland, Macoun." Then we discover the 'Honeycrisp,' the featured apple of the week. They are huge, the size of small grapefruits, green with gorgeous red streaks. These apples have so much crunch that it's not an exaggeration to say it's a noisy experience biting into one. Serious snap. I'm not sure they are the ones I want to pick (my latest obsession is with the green, slightly spicy apples called 'Ginger Golds'). But one bite of the Honey Crisps and I'm hooked. They drip a sweet elixir that tastes like it's been laced with freshly ground cinnamon.

Driving home, we talk about pies and tarts, apple cakes and strudels. But we decide we want to make a big batch of applesauce in an attempt to capture the apple's honey-like juice and preserve it well into winter.

Meanwhile, my older daughter and a close friend of hers are home for the weekend. We enlist their help first thing the next morning. (First thing in the morning for a twenty-something home for the weekend is around noon.) Well rested, they peel the fruit with a vengeance and before I know it there are twenty pounds of naked apples on the table. They bite into them and scream: "How can an apple be this sweet and juicy?" I think about the little girl with the white stained dress. I think about how my daughter was that little girl just a mega-second ago. I think about how time plays strange tricks on us all.

My daughter's friend has German relatives and her German vocabulary includes the word *apfelmus*, meaning applesauce. As she peels, she chants: "Let's make *apfelmus*." Soon we are all laughing and saying the word *apfelmus* as much as possible.

But when I suggest to my daughter and our friends that we roast the applesauce instead of doing the traditional long simmer, they look at me the way my dog does when I say something really confusing.

I explain that I'd done some experimenting the previous fall and that roasting apples is a terrific, undiscovered technique. "All we do is peel the apples, toss them with some spices and a touch of sugar, and they naturally caramelize and cook down on their own. Then you simply mash them with a potato masher when they come out of the oven all hot and gooey and . . . instant applesauce." At this point their expression changes: it now says "You must be a genius or something!"

We pull out my biggest roasting pan, toss the apples with ground cinnamon, ginger, a touch of cardamom, allspice, maple syrup, and sugar. We put the apples into the hot oven and walk away. We go outside and walk through the woods. When we get back, the kitchen smells like a cliché of fall — crisp and full of apples pie and spices. You can practically imagine a thick sweater and a roaring fire. I take the pan out of the oven and mash the apples lightly and then we taste.

My daughter starts chanting, "This is the best *apfelmus* I've ever tasted," and her friend repeats over and over "Mmmm, *apfelmus*." We put some of the *apfelmus* into jars and some of it into bags for the freezer and go back outside to watch the leaves do their color dance.

# Roasted *Apfelmus* (Applesauce)

Go apple picking and pick as many varieties of apples as you can find. It's nice to mix super-sweet ones with sour ones, firm with soft. You can also mix some peeled, cored, and chopped seasonal pears.

Preheat the oven to 450 degrees.

Peel and core the apples and cut them into 1-inch slices. Place them in a large roasting pan and mix with maple syrup (about 1/4 cup for every three pounds of apples). Sprinkle on a heavy dash of any or all of the following spices: cinnamon, cardamom, nutmeg, allspice, and ground ginger. Mix well, sprinkle on about 1/8 cup sugar for every three pounds (depending on how sweet you like your applesauce, you can add more or less, or none at all).

Place the roasting pan on the middle shelf in the preheated oven and cover with foil. Roast for 30 minutes. Stir gently after 30 minutes. Uncover and add 1/2 to 1 cup apple cider (for every three pounds of apples), and roast another 30 to 45 minutes or until the apples are very tender and just starting to fall apart and burst.

Remove from the oven and let cool a few minutes before using a potato masher to gently mash the apples to the consistency you like your applesauce: thick and chunky or smooth. Taste for seasoning, and add more sugar or spice if needed. Place in a bowl or covered jar and refrigerate for up to 5 to 7 days, or place in freezer bags, seal tightly, and freeze for up to 6 months.

# Baked Spiced Apple-Raisin Pancakes

A simple pancake batter is poured over apple slices that have been sautéed with spices and raisins and baked in a hot oven. You serve the pancakes straight from the skillet with warm maple syrup poured on top.

*Serves 2 to 4*

### For the batter:

1/2 cup flour
1 tablespoon sugar
1 pinch salt
2 eggs
1/2 cup (2%) milk
1 tablespoon safflower or canola oil
1/8 teaspoon ground cinnamon
1/8 teaspoon ground nutmeg

### For the apples:

1 tablespoon unsalted butter
2 medium-large apples, peeled, cored, and cut into 12 thin slices
1/3 cup raisins
1/4 cup maple syrup
1/8 teaspoon ground cinnamon
1/8 teaspoon ground nutmeg
warm maple syrup, for serving

Preheat the oven to 475 degrees.

In a large bowl, mix the flour, sugar, and salt. In a small bowl, whisk the eggs and the milk. Add the egg mixture to the flour and stir in the oil, cinnamon, and nutmeg.

Heat the butter over moderate heat in a 10-inch ovenproof skillet. Add the apples and cook for 3 minutes. Add the raisins, maple syrup, cinnamon, and nutmeg, and cook for another 2 to 3 minutes, or until the apples have softened and are coated in the syrup and spices.

Remove the apples from the heat and press them down into a single layer. Pour the batter on top and place on the middle shelf of the oven. Bake for 10 to 11 minutes, or until the pancake is puffed on the sides and looks cooked in the center. Remove and serve immediately with warm maple syrup on the side.

# Grilled Gruyère Sandwiches *with* Maple-Caramelized Apples

I like serving this sandwich open-faced for breakfast with cups of strong coffee or for lunch with a seasonal salad. The two sandwich halves (on crusty baguette or slices of your favorite bread) can be served open-faced or they can be put together to make a more traditional-style sandwich. You can also use pears to give this sandwich a twist.

*Serves 2 to 4*

### For the apples:

1 teaspoon salted butter
1 teaspoon olive or safflower oil
1 tart apple, peeled, cored, and thinly sliced
1 1/2 tablespoons maple syrup

### For the sandwich:

two (4-inch) pieces of baguette or crusty bread, cut in half lengthwise,
    or 4 slices of your favorite bread
2 1/2 ounces very thinly sliced Gruyère cheese

In a medium skillet, heat the butter and oil over low heat. When sizzling, add the apple slices and cook, stirring gently once or twice, for 3 minutes. Drizzle on the maple syrup and raise the heat to medium-high. Cook for another 2 minutes, or until the apples are caramelized and just tender, but not mushy. Remove from the heat.

Preheat the broiler.

Place the bread on a small broiler pan. Divide the apples and the syrup in the bottom of the skillet between the four pieces of bread. Place the cheese on top of the apples and place the bread under the broiler. Broil for 2 to 3 minutes, or until the cheese is bubbling and melted.

# FALL IS CIDER TIME

I t's spitting a kind of wet, slushy mush. But when friends down the street have their annual Apple Cider Pressing Party, people show up no matter what the weather. There's something about the fall and apples and pressing cider that makes New Englanders happy. Maybe it's because we know, deep inside, that this is the last harvest, the final bit of local sweetness before the frost takes over and freezes the earth. Or maybe it's just that apples and apple cider are so incredibly delicious.

Our friends use a hand-crank wooden press, the kind that takes a good bit of muscle and man and woman power to operate. Everyone brings their own apples — from their trees or a neighbor's — along with some sweet local pears, and we begin pressing. Every batch of cider combines several varieties of apples, each adding its own bit of sweetness and spice. The complex flavors — cinnamon, sugar, maple, and a hint of nutmeg — that are released from the press strike me as perfectly balanced, like a well-made wine. The texture, slightly thick and syrupy, is equally pleasing with its smooth, velvety feel. A glass of freshly pressed cider is like drinking a whole season of autumn one sip at a time.

As we stand around that cold, wet barn, taking turns cranking the press and throwing apples into the chute, the talk inevitably turns to cooking. "I like throwing cider into the pan when I'm sautéing pork chops," one woman told me. "I add it to my applesauce every year," announces another. "We like mixing it with dark rum and fresh lime juice," one guy chimes in. "I mix it into my pancake and waffle batter," said the mother of two little girls clinging to her legs. "Sunday morning apple pancakes. Use it instead of milk in your pancake recipe."

And then I innocently mention that I like to boil down a jug of cider to make jelly. The room goes kind of quiet. "Jelly?" someone asks "Sure," I answer and explain the recipe. Boil a quart of cider for three long hours and eventually you are left with a thick, amber-colored jelly. Real simple. "Wow!" a few people mumble, "Way cool!" Everyone goes back to sipping cider, exchanging recipes, and trying to keep warm. I take my jug of cider (a party favor for each guest) home and start boiling.

# Apple Cider Jelly

There are some recipes that seem to have more in common with magic than plain old everyday cooking. Apples have lots of natural pectin, so one October day I wondered what would happen if I simmered down an entire gallon of good apple cider? The answer: You are left with a gorgeous, amber-colored, natural apple cider jelly. The only catch — this is true *slow* cooking — it can take up to three hours to transform one gallon of cider into about a cup of jelly, but trust me when I say it's well worth the time.

Making apple cider jelly is a great project when you're in the kitchen busy baking cookies or other holiday foods.

Serve the jelly as a condiment with holiday roasts — we particularly like it with roast pork, turkey, chicken, lamb, and beef — or on your morning muffins and toast, with squash dishes, and even on top of butter cookies. It's excellent on a sharp cheddar cheese sandwich. Make a few batches and give the cider jelly as a gift.

*Makes about 1 cup*

**one gallon unpasteurized apple cider, with no additives**

Place the cider in a large, heavy pot and bring to a gentle boil over high heat. Reduce the heat to low and let simmer for about 2 hours. After about 2 hours the cider will begin to thicken and coat the back of a spoon. This is the time to pay attention. *Do not answer the phone — stay focused on the jelly.* Keep cooking over a gentle simmer, on very low heat, for another 45 minutes or until the jam begins to thicken and the syrupy mixture comes to about 190 degrees on a candy thermometer. My jelly took almost three hours to thicken. Let cool and place in a glass jelly jar. Refrigerate. The jelly will keep for several weeks.

## Variations:

• For a spicy jelly: place a chile pepper cut in half down the middle into a piece of cheesecloth and tie it up. Place the chile into the cider for the first hour of cooking, and then remove.

• Make a mulled cider jelly: place a cinnamon stick, allspice berries, and three cloves in a piece of cheesecloth and tie it up tightly. Place in the jelly during the first hour of cooking, and then remove.

• For an herbal apple cider jelly: place several leaves of fresh sage, rosemary, and oregano (or any fresh herb) in a piece of cheesecloth and tie up tightly. Place in the cider for the first 1½ hours of cooking time, and then remove.

# November

# HUNGER IN MAINE

When my older daughter was in first grade, I volunteered in her classroom from time to time. One morning a girl was interrupting the teacher, acting out, and creating chaos. The teacher asked me if I would take her outside the classroom and keep an eye on her. As we sat in the hallway, she wept. I asked her what was going on, why she was so sad? She looked at me and sobbed. "I didn't have dinner last night, and I didn't get any breakfast this morning, and I'm just so, so hungry." It was one of those moments when time stops, for just a second, and the world as you know it is not the same. I gave the girl a tissue and asked her to explain. "My mom said we don't have any money for food until next month."

I told the girl to wait there while I went inside and spoke to the teacher. I explained the situation and watched the color drain from her always cheerful first-grade-teacher face. She ransacked the cabinets and came up with an apple, crackers, and peanut butter, while I raided my daughter's lunch box. The girl ate everything quietly, downing every last crumb. I left her money for school lunch and the teacher promised me she would make sure the girl got a hot lunch at school every day.

For the first time, I was face to face with hunger in America, in Maine. I understood that hunger was not just an issue in far-away lands where people deal with drought, famine, and poverty. It was a day I never forgot.

That experience still haunts me. Soon after, I learned about a group looking for help at a local soup kitchen. As a food writer and cookbook author who spends an inordinate amount of time thinking about food, I decided it was time to start feeding people who were not there to judge my culinary abilities, but who show up because they are just plain hungry.

Several times a year, together with a group of volunteers, I cook dinner at the soup kitchen. As the economy becomes more and more challenging, the number of people who eat there grows each month. It turns out that in 2010, Maine's rate of childhood hunger was the highest in New England. More than 2 percent of Maine's children face "food insecurity." That translates to thousands of kids across the state who don't have enough to eat.

When I first started work at the soup kitchen, I used the supplies they had in the pantry. I tried to make the most of the boxed mashed potatoes and biscuit mix, generic hamburger meat, canned corn, and supermarket cakes. But it didn't feel right. I didn't like cooking and serving food that I wouldn't serve to my own family and friends.

So, after a while, I started doing the shopping myself and cooking the kind of simple, comforting, and fresh foods I'd be proud to serve at home. Why would I do anything less for people who *really* need it?

I've simmered huge pots of homemade tomato sauce to spoon over double-dipped chicken Parmesan, roasted pork with local apples and pears, and cooked up spaghetti and meatballs, three-cheese mac-and-cheese, smoked ham glazed with maple syrup, mashed Maine potatoes, steamed carrots, crusty garlic bread, and seasonal salads.

T he church social hall fills around 4 P.M. Some come with young children and babies, others sit alone, staring off into the distance. Many try to make themselves invisible. They are here out of need, and they are not proud of it. A volunteer plays jazz on a piano in the corner. Sometimes he is accompanied by a singer who croons "Blue Moon" and other standards. The music gives a little warmth to the bare-bones room with its round tables and plastic tablecloths. When the meal is served — at 5 P.M. sharp — the conversation starts flowing.

We pass around bowls of fresh tossed salad, offering fresh vegetables to people who can't afford them or won't buy them because they don't know how to cook them. Then dinner is served, accompanied by rolls or garlic bread, and finally dessert. The room fills gradually over the hour and a half that we offer dinner, and we never know if we'll feed thirty people or one hundred and thirty. Plates are filled generously. I always cook more than we need because I want to have plenty of leftovers. My goal is to be able to offer take-home food to the families, particularly the ones with small children. It breaks my heart if I let myself think about what they might, or might not, have eaten if we hadn't cooked for them.

One night, just after we had finished cooking and were beginning to clean up, one of the diners asked to speak to the person who made the macaroni and cheese. The fifty-something man wore a frayed checked flannel shirt, jeans, and had a stubbly beard. I hoped there wasn't going to be trouble. "There's something wrong with that mac and cheese," he said, looking me directly in the eye. "There's some kind of s'more in it." I was confused and asked him to repeat it. "There's s'more in it. When you eat it, it makes you want s'more and s'more and s'more." A group of men at a nearby table laughed uncontrollably. "Yeah," one of them yelled over to me, "Excellent stuff!"

Then there was the time I served roasted vegetable soup. A guy in a T-shirt and knitted cap with a large hole in the center came to the kitchen door. "I don't know how to cook," he said, "and I don't know how to make soup. But I'll tell you something. If I could make soup, I'd want it to taste just like that. I felt like crap when I got here. I feel really good now!" I choked back tears and thanked him.

When anyone asks why I bother to peel fresh carrots and roast them with Maine maple syrup or peel dozens of potatoes to mash instead of opening a box of potato flakes, I think of that man. I think of the young mother, clutching the hands of her two wide-eyed toddlers, who thanked me for the bag of leftovers. "This will get us through the next day or two." I handed her an extra portion because the look in those children's eyes let me know just how important that food really was to them.

My work at the soup kitchen always left me wanting to do more. The answer came to me during the spring of 2010 when First Lady Michelle Obama announced a program called Let's Move, an initiative to combat childhood obesity and improve the quality of the food served in American public-school cafeterias. She invited chefs from around the country to come to the White House. Their assignment? Adopt a school in their community and try to improve the food served in that school. The idea sounded like grass roots activism at its best.

As a young girl my fantasy was to meet Julie Andrews; as a teen my dreams veered to Mick Jagger. These days there are few people I would rather meet than the Obamas. Apparently more than eight hundred chefs shared my interest, because that's how many showed up to be part of the Chefs Move to Schools campaign.

The lawn of the White House is a glorious place. Gone was the noise of traffic, police cars, helicopters, and the city buzz was replaced by birds and the smell of roses. (Oh my, the Rose Garden. The Rose Garden.) We walked around the gardens, taking photos, and feeling the intense excitement.

The First Lady spoke about the connection between food and happiness. "So many good memories involve food," she said. "You are all at the heart of this initiative because if anyone understands nutrition and food, it's the folks sitting here in their whites today. You know more about food than almost anyone — other than the grandmas — and you've got the visibility and the enthusiasm to match that knowledge." She talked about how many children go to school hungry and how school lunches were so crucial to their nutrition. I thought about the hungry girl in my daughter's first-grade class and how, in a way, she was responsible for my being at the White House.

Mrs. Obama urged us all to go home and make friends with the principal and teachers. "Bring them food," she joked, "and they will welcome you. Expect people to say no," Mrs. Obama warned. "Everyone will tell you there's no money, and they don't have the time to help. But be patient!"

What happened in the ensuing weeks was exactly the opposite of what Mrs. Obama warned. I came home and contacted the principal at the local elementary school in town. She started breathing heavily when I mentioned my trip to the White House. "This is so exciting," she enthused. "Let's make this happen!" She is one of those dream principals who cares so much about the kids that she is often seen in her office past dark each night.

I met with the PTO and all sorts of people — mothers, fathers, teachers — who offered to volunteer their time and effort. A landscape architect, a farmer, and several members of the school board all offered their services. A parent found someone willing to donate a hoop house.

As I write, this project is at the very beginning stages. I asked the kids to come up with a name for the project. We made a contest of it. All the first, second, and third graders sat quietly (incredibly quietly). It was like watching the sunrise — their faces lit up as I described the project. I explained to them what a hoop house was and how we would build one in the backyard behind their school, and I told them we would grow vegetables in there — even during the cold months.

They all shouted out the name of their favorite vegetables, and carrots seemed to be the overwhelming favorite. I also heard tomatoes, broccoli, and corn. I told them I would be coming into their classrooms, cooking with them, and talking about nutrition and all the delicious ways there are to eat fruits and vegetables. The excitement was palpable. Despite the late-summer heat, I left the building with chills.

When the school assembly was all over, a little boy told his teacher he just *had* to meet me. He came up and we shook hands. "I am really good at building things, and I want to help build the hoop house," he told me, a shy grin spreading across his face. "We can do it. This is gonna be super cool."

My dream is that one day, despite the long, cold Maine winters, the kids will grow enough fruits and vegetables that can be served in their own cafeteria. My dream is that the teachers will use the garden as an extended classroom, and work out a curriculum that uses gardening and the planting and growing of vegetables to help teach writing, art, history, math, and science. My dream is that one day kids will know what it means to eat food fresh from the ground, from the tree, from the vine, and not just from the freezer or plastic pouch. My dream, like Michelle Obama's, is that one day the food found in our school cafeterias will have color, freshness, and will actually be good for children. My dreams are *very slowly* beginning to come true.

163

# Four Cheese Macaroni *with* Thyme–Parmesan Crust

Trust me, this is not your ordinary mac and cheese. When you add fresh mozzarella, Fontina, Parmesan, and crème fraîche to pasta, something out of the ordinary happens. You can also add a layer of fresh mozzarella in the middle of the pasta dish for the ultimate cheese experience, and scatter a mixture of grated Parmesan, thyme, and breadcrumbs on top for a crunchy topping. You can make the dish in one large skillet, or baking dish, or make it in individual ramekins, but you'll need to reduce the baking time. The dish can be assembled up to 2 hours ahead of time and baked just before serving. And, when you're cooking for a crowd, simply double or triple the recipe into individual batches. You can also add a layer of sautéed crumbled sausage to the middle layer of the casserole.

*Serves 6 to 8*

>   2 tablespoons olive oil
>   1 tablespoon unsalted butter
>   3 tablespoons flour
>   3 cups milk, warmed
>   2 cups grated fresh mozzarella cheese
>   1 cup freshly grated Parmesan cheese
>   1 cup grated Fontina cheese
>   1/4 cup crème fraîche or sour cream
>   salt and freshly ground pepper
>   2 tablespoons plus 2 teaspoons chopped fresh thyme leaves
>   1 pound macaroni or short textured pasta like cavatappi, ziti rigate, or penne rigate
>   1/2 cup plain breadcrumbs
>   1/2 teaspoon Hungarian paprika

Place a rack in the middle of the oven and preheat oven to 400 degrees.

Melt the butter and 1 tablespoon of the olive oil in a medium saucepan over low heat. When the butter has melted completely and begins to sizzle, add the flour and whisk until combined. Cook, stirring constantly, until the mixture begins to bubble, 1 to 2 minutes. Add half of the warm milk in a slow, steady stream, whisking until the mixture is smooth and begins to thicken, about 2 minutes. Add the remaining milk, whisk again until smooth, and increase the heat to medium–high, stirring frequently, until the mixture comes to a simmer. Reduce the heat to low and cook until the sauce is just about thick enough to coat the back of a spoon. Remove the sauce from heat and add half of the mozzarella and half of the Parmesan, and all of the Fontina and crème fraîche, whisking constantly to prevent the cheese from becoming lumpy. When the sauce is completely smooth, add salt and pepper to taste and 2 tablespoons of the thyme.

Meanwhile, bring a large pot of lightly salted water to boil over high heat. Add the pasta and cook until just tender, or *al dente*, 7 to 9 minutes. Drain, return to the pot, and set aside.

Pour the sauce over the pasta in the pot and stir to combine completely. Spoon half of the pasta into a large ovenproof skillet, or a roughly 9 x 12-inch baking dish or several smaller dishes (ramekins work really well), and arrange the remaining mozzarella evenly over the pasta. Pour the remaining pasta over the cheese layer and spread evenly.

Mix the remaining Parmesan cheese, the remaining 2 teaspoons thyme, the breadcrumbs, and the paprika together in a small bowl. Sprinkle the mixture evenly over the top of the pasta. Drizzle the remaining tablespoon olive oil evenly over the crust.

Bake the pasta for 20 to 30 minutes (smaller dishes will bake in 15 to 20 minutes), or until the pasta is hot, the cheese is bubbly, and the crust is golden brown.

### Tip

*Dont' throw out that rind! When making mac and cheese or pasta or anything that calls for Parmesan cheese, I never throw away the rind. Parmesan cheese rind adds great flavor to soups and sauces, and can also act as a natural thickener for sauces. There's still a lot of flavor left in the rind, so don't throw it away.*

## Leek, Potato, *and* Sharp Cheddar Cheese Soup *with* Chive–Walnut–Cheddar Swirl

Leeks and potatoes are good companions, and here they are joined by the sharpness of cheddar. This is pure comfort food, smooth, rich, and bursting with flavor. The Chive-Walnut-Cheddar Swirl is added to the soup at the table, highlighting the smooth white soup with a gorgeous green color and a cheesy, herby, nutty flavor and texture. This soup makes a great first course for any holiday feast, or can be served as a meal on its own with crusty bread and a mixed green salad. Be sure to choose a really distinctive, very sharp cheddar for this soup.

*Serves 6 to 12*

### For the soup:

2 tablespoons olive oil

2 pounds leeks, washed, ends trimmed, and all green sections discarded, whites only, cut lengthwise and then into thin slices

2½ pounds potatoes, peeled and chopped

salt and freshly ground white or black pepper, to taste

7 cups chicken or vegetable stock, homemade or a good, organic variety of canned or boxed

¾ to 1 cup grated sharp cheddar cheese

### For the Chive–Walnut–Cheddar Swirl:

1 cup fresh chives, chopped

⅓ cup walnut halves

salt and freshly ground black pepper, to taste

½ cup olive oil

½ cup grated sharp cheddar cheese

Prepare the soup: in a large soup pot, heat the oil over low heat. Add the leeks, cover, and cook, stirring once or twice, for 10 minutes. Add the potatoes and cook, stirring them to coat with the leeks and oil, for 3 minutes. Season with salt and pepper. Add the stock, raise the heat to high, and bring the mixture to a boil. Once the soup comes to a boil, reduce the heat to low, cover, and cook for about 20 minutes, or until the potatoes are perfectly tender and the broth is flavorful.

Let the soup cool slightly. Using a hand-held immersion blender, or transferring the soup to a blender or food processor, puree the soup until completely smooth. Place the soup back into the pot (if using a food processor or blender) and sprinkle in the cheese. Heat over low heat and taste for seasoning.

Make the swirl: in the container of a food processor, pulse the chives and walnuts until well chopped. Add salt and pepper and the oil and process until well blended; the mixture will be thick and chunky. Add the cheese and pulse several times to incorporate. Taste for seasoning and adjust as needed. The swirl can be made several hours ahead of time; cover and refrigerate.

To serve, place the soup in a serving bowl and swirl in a generous teaspoon or two of the Chive-Walnut-Cheddar Swirl. Serve hot.

# Roast Pork *with* Apples *and* Pears

Thin slices of apples and pears are lined on the bottom of a large roasting pan and pork chops (or a pork roast) is placed on top, sprinkled with fresh thyme, rosemary, sage, and fresh apple cider and roasted until the meat is tender and the fruit breaks down into a natural apple-pear sauce. You can easily double or triple this recipe.

*Serves 2 to 4*

> 1 tablespoon olive oil
> 2 tart apples, peeled, cored, and cut into thin slices
> 2 ripe pears, peeled, cored, and cut into thin slices
> salt and freshly ground black pepper
> 1 tablespoon chopped fresh sage
> 1 tablespoon chopped fresh thyme
> 1 tablespoon chopped fresh rosemary
> 4 pork rib chops, about ¾ to 1 inch thick
> ½ cup apple cider with no preservatives

Preheat the oven to 400 degrees.

Spread the oil along the bottom of medium-size roasting pan or ovenproof skillet. Place the apple and pear slices on top and season with the salt, pepper, and half the sage, thyme, and rosemary. Place the pork chops on top of the fruit, sprinkle with salt, pepper, and the remaining herbs. Pour the cider on top. Place on the middle shelf and roast for 15 minutes. Baste the pork with the cider, adding more if it seems like the pan is drying out at all. Roast for 5 to 10 additional minutes, or until the internal temperature of the meat, when tested with an instant-read meat thermometer, reaches 150 degrees. The apples and pears should be broken down and soft. Remove from the oven and cover loosely with foil; the temperature will rise to 155 degrees. Serve the chops hot with the apple-pear sauce and any juices poured on top.

### Tip

*You can also use half apple cider and half pineapple juice for a really interesting fruit flavor.*

# A NEW LOOK AT THANKSGIVING

There's something to be said for rituals. Turkey signals Thanksgiving, but in our house so does cranberry sauce (homemade with pineapple, pecans, and fresh ginger, as well as the canned variety; *page 172*), oyster and bread stuffing, mashed potatoes with roasted garlic (*page 81*), not to mention creamed spinach (*page 82*), and pureed squash. Pecan pie, cranberry cheesecake, pumpkin pie. Ah, yes, there is real safety in tradition, but sometimes the cook in me feels rebellious and wants to break out.

Why might I veer away from my mother-in-law's famed and infamous Jello mold (made with crushed canned pineapple and orange sherbet)? Why would I want to introduce new flavors — like blood orange and fresh ginger — to the pureed squash? Why might I make a pumpkin brittle (*page 182*) to crumble on top of our salad, with local blue cheese and tiny cubes of tangerine?

Sure, it's fun to shake things up a bit, but there's also a deeper, more profound reason I need to make Thanksgiving a bit different. My family is changing. My daughters are not always here for Thanksgiving any more — sometimes we gather around the table with a wonderful combination of family and old friends. One daughter is with friends and the other is overseas. My mother-in-law often spends the holiday in California with my sister-in-law, instead of sticking to the usual tradition of joining us here in Maine. These absences create huge gaps at our table — both physical and emotional.

Each year when we gather at the table, I am acutely aware of who is there and who is missing. My mother and father have been gone for years now, but, as the years go by, their presence at the holiday table grows stronger for me. I see them and feel them when I look into my daughter's eyes, when we set the table with the silverware my mother left me, in the special dishes we always made together.

One of our holiday traditions is to go around the table and have everyone say something they are grateful for. I always say "I am so grateful for my family and friends and my health," or some version of that sentiment. And then, almost immediately, I keep to tradition and wipe away my unwanted, but always-predictable, flood of tears (while my younger daughter shakes her head in embarrassment and sighs "Mom!").

You might think that the more things change the more I want to stick to tradition (in an attempt to try to fool myself into thinking that everything is the same). But I know things are shifting, so it feels right to shake things up when it comes to the food served at our holiday feast.

We will have turkey (I'm not that much of a rebel!), but it will be grilled. I know this doesn't sound revolutionary, but trust me — with this clan it is. Several years ago, when I was testing recipes for a grilling book, I decided to try grilling a whole turkey. I figured it might be a good idea, but worried the meat would dry out. Not only did grilling the bird turn out to be one of the simplest recipes I experimented with, it was also one of the juiciest, tenderest, most successful turkeys I've ever cooked.

The beauty of grilling a turkey is two-fold: it frees up the oven for all those fabulous side dishes you want to keep warm, and it forces you outside and into the fresh air — even on a cold, miserable November day.

There were some protests when I mentioned I would be grilling the holiday bird, so I was "forced" to roast a second bird in the oven as well. The consensus was that the grilled bird was every bit as good as the traditional roasted one. (Some people, who shall remain nameless, had trouble admitting that the grilled turkey was actually better — juicier, crisper skin, perfectly cooked.)

The thing about rituals and traditions is that they provide a context, but it doesn't mean everything is written in stone. I love celebrating this feast year after year, and I love keeping much of it the same year after year. But not all of it. Rebel a little this year. See what happens. It just may surprise you.

# Grilled Turkey

Don't wait until Thanksgiving to try this recipe. It's a great dish for a crowd year-round.

> one (10- to 14-pound) turkey
> salt
> freshly ground black pepper
> 1 tablespoon finely chopped rosemary, thyme, or sage
> 1 tablespoon chopped garlic

Clean the turkey and remove the giblets and liver. Dry thoroughly. Place the salt, pepper, herbs, and garlic in the cavity and on top of the bird.

Next, make the fire. You will be grilling the turkey whole using a method called "indirect grilling." If working with a charcoal grill, heat a good amount of charcoal until hot. Spread the coals on either side of the grill, leaving the middle part of the grill without any charcoal under it. If working with a gas grill, preheat the grill to 450 degrees and turn off the burner directly in the center, or on one side, of the grill. When you place your hand over the grill grate it should feel *very* hot. No matter what method you're using, place a disposable aluminum drip pan directly under the center of the grill – it will be used to catch the juices and fat that drip off the bird as it cooks and not create a mess of your grill.

Place the bird in the middle of the grill, in the area where it doesn't have direct heat underneath. Cover and cook 2 to 2½ hours or until the juices in the cavity are no longer pink and when the drumstick is jiggled gently it feels loose. You don't need to baste the bird or do a thing. (I told you this was simple!) The turkey will cook faster than it will when roasted normally in an oven, so keep an eye on it, particularly during the last 30 minutes of the grilling time. Look for a deeply colored, crispy brown skin. A 10- to 14-pound bird will feed 10 to 14 people, but leftovers are crucial, so figure a pound per person.

# Cranberry Sauce *with* Orange, Ginger, Pineapple, *and* Pecans

Every year I tweak my holiday cranberry sauce just a bit, but this combination (tart berries with sweet oranges, ginger, pineapple chunks, and meaty pecans) is a real favorite. Serve with holiday poultry, on sandwiches, with a cheese platter, or serve it as a dessert sauce for butter cookies, pound cake, or pies.

*Makes about 6 cups*

> 1 cup sugar
> 2 cups water
> ¼ cup maple syrup
> 1 pound fresh cranberries
> ¼ cup fresh orange juice
> ¼ cup julienned orange rind
> 1 tablespoon grated orange zest
> 1 tablespoon finely chopped fresh ginger
> 1 tablespoon coarsely chopped candied (or crystallized) ginger
> 1 cup pecans, or your favorite nut, coarsely chopped

Place the sugar and water in a large saucepan and bring to a boil over high heat. Reduce the heat to low and cook 10 to 15 minutes, or until the sugar syrup beings to thicken slightly and turn a pale amber color. Add the maple syrup and the cranberries and cook, stirring occasionally, until the cranberries begin to pop. Add the orange juice, orange rind, and orange zest and cook another 5 to 10 minutes, or until the sauce beings to thicken *slightly*. Add the fresh and crystallized ginger and cook 2 minutes. The sauce should be full of flavor and slightly thickened. (If the sauce still seems thin — remember, it will thicken as it chills — remove the cranberries and flavorings with a slotted spoon and place in a bowl. Boil the liquid in the pot over a moderate-high heat until it is thickened slightly, about 10 additional minutes, if needed. Place the cranberries back in the slightly thickened sauce.)

Remove the sauce from the heat and add the nuts, stirring well. Let cool completely. Place in a clean glass jar and cover; refrigerate for up 10 days, or freeze for up to 6 months.

### Tip

*You'll need 2 to 3 large oranges. First, use one orange to remove the zest (the outer peel without the bitter white pith) by slicing it off with a small sharp knife or a wide vegetable peeler. Use another orange to grate the rind and then squeeze both oranges for their juice.*

# Turkey Stock

When the long, heavy Thanksgiving weekend has ended, we all let out a collective sigh of relief. I don't know about you, but all that rich food makes me awfully sleepy. One of my just-after-Thanksgiving rituals is taking the turkey carcass (after several days of leftovers I don't even want to look at turkey meat for a while) and simmering up a soup. Be sure to trim all the meat off your turkey carcass (you can freeze it, make a pot pie, sandwiches, etc.). The stock can be placed in containers or tightly sealed plastic bags and frozen for up to six months. Be sure to label the stock with the date you froze it.

*Makes about 10 cups stock*

1 turkey carcass, anywhere from 10 to 20 pounds
2 large onions, chopped
2 leeks, trimmed, washed, and chopped
4 carrots, chopped
4 ribs celery, chopped
6 peppercorns
2 bay leaves
1/3 cup finely chopped fresh parsley with the stems
salt and freshly ground black pepper to taste

Place the turkey carcass in a large soup or stock pot and cover with 10 to 12 cups of cold water (the carcass should be *almost* fully covered with water, so add more if you need to). Add the onions, leeks, carrots, celery, peppercorns, bay leaves, parsley, salt, and pepper. Bring to a boil over high heat, reduce the heat to low, and let simmer, partially covered, for 1 1/2 to 2 hours, or until the stock is really flavorful. If the stock still tastes weak, bring it to a rolling boil uncovered and let cook another 15 to 20 minutes until reduced and flavorful.

Let cool slightly, strain, and use the stock for soup *(page 174)*. Freeze for up to 6 months, or cover and refrigerate for up to 5 days.

# Greek-Style Turkey-Lemon-Rice Soup

This is one of my favorite ways to use leftover turkey and turkey stock (you can also use chicken stock or canned chicken stock, but there's something about that turkey flavor that makes it even better) after the holidays. The soup is pure, unadulterated comfort food.

*Serves 6 to 8*

8 cups turkey broth, or chicken broth
1/2 cup fresh parsley, finely chopped
2 tablespoons chopped fresh thyme
2 cups cooked white rice, at room temperature
2 cups cooked turkey or chicken, chopped into bite-size pieces
2 egg yolks
1/3 cup heavy cream, optional
salt and freshly ground black pepper
juice from 3 large lemons, about 1/2 cup
1 lemon, preferably organic, scrubbed and cut into paper-thin slices
       with the seeds removed

Place the turkey broth in a large pot and bring to a simmer over moderately high heat. Reduce the heat to low and add half the parsley and all of the thyme. Add the rice to the soup, making sure to break up any clumps. Add the turkey and simmer over *very low* heat.

In a small bowl, whisk the egg yolks and cream (if using any) with a good amount of salt and pepper. Add about 1/2 cup of the hot broth to the bowl and whisk with the yolks. Add the yolk mixture back to the pot and whisk until fully incorporated. Add the lemon juice and season to taste. It is important that you don't let the soup boil; if it does, the egg yolks will cook and you simply want to whisk the soup back to smoothness. Taste for seasoning and add more salt, pepper, or lemon juice as needed. Keep in mind that the longer the soup sits, the thicker it will become; add more broth if necessary.

Serve hot with a slice of lemon and a sprinkling of parsley in each bowl.

# GARLIC: ONE LAST, LATE PLANTING

There are still leeks, Brussels sprouts, onions, shallots, carrots, and beets in the garden. It's surprising that this many crops can hold on until November, an encouraging sign that growing seasons are lasting longer than they used to. And, despite the terrifying realities of global warming, I couldn't be happier. It's always hard to say goodbye to the garden, and give in to the impending darkness and cold. But, surrounded by these gorgeous root vegetables that thrive despite the ever-increasing cold nights, I am ready to believe in cycles and seasons and changing temperatures. What choice do I really have?

The earth is still soft enough to dig easily. I pile on some well-seasoned compost and make several long rows. I'm planting three varieties of garlic that a friend brought me from the Common Ground Country Fair this past September. I separate the firm cloves from the garlic heads and push them, root side down, into the cool earth. I cover them up well, like patting a child beneath their favorite quilt, and wish them a good winter. "See you in the spring," I tell them, well aware that I am talking to cloves of garlic.

175

# Roasted Garlic Bread

You can prepare this garlic bread several hours ahead of time and pop it in the oven about 10 minutes before serving. This is a great treat for a holiday meal or any family dinner. Instead of using garlic butter, try the Ramp Butter *(page 68)*.

*Serves 4 to 6*

> 1 head of garlic, with a thin slice cut off the top to just expose the cloves
> 2½ tablespoons olive oil
> 2 tablespoons salted butter
> 1 tablespoon chopped fresh thyme
> freshly ground black pepper
> 1 crusty baguette or French- or Italian-style bread

Preheat the oven to 350 degrees. Place the garlic in a small ovenproof skillet or pan and pour the oil on top. Roast for about 15 minutes. To check the garlic, squeeze the cloves; they should feel soft but not mushy. Roast another 5 minutes if needed, remove from the oven, and let cool slightly.

When cool enough to handle, squeeze the garlic out of its skin and chop coarsely. Be sure to save the oil in the bottom of the pan that you roasted the garlic in.

Meanwhile, in a small skillet or saucepan, heat the butter over low heat. Add the thyme, pepper, and the oil from the roasted garlic pan. Add the chopped roasted garlic and let simmer for 2 minutes. Remove from the heat.

Cut the bread into ½-inch-wide slices on the diagonal; line the slices up to recreate the shape of the loaf on a long piece of aluminum foil. Using a pastry brush or a small spoon, divide the butter (and garlic) between each slice of bread, recreating the shape of the loaf again. Brush any remaining butter on top of the bread. Seal the foil tightly. (The bread can be made several hours ahead of time up to this point. Refrigerate or keep in a cool spot.)

Preheat the oven to 400 degrees. Bake the bread for 10 to 12 minutes, or until it is hot and the butter is warm. Serve hot.

# December

# HOLIDAY ENTERTAINING WITHOUT PROZAC

Here's the way things work around here. My husband, John, clever man that he is, knows that when we entertain I like to get things just right. "Just right" means different things to different people, but when I give a party, expectations are high, both mine and those of my guests. This is never truer than around the holidays, when the pressure to entertain reaches a fever pitch, as does my resistance to entertaining. Since I write cookbooks for a living, people come to our house to be dazzled by the food I serve. It's not that I don't want to dazzle them. But sometimes I'd rather just cook a simple meal and be done with it.

So here's what John does. We are about to go away for the holidays, and on December 19 or 20 he says, oh so casually, "Why don't we have a little end-of-the-year/beginning-of-the-New-Year celebration when we get home?" It sounds innocent enough, but trust me there is nothing innocent about it. He gives me that endearing little smile — the one that makes him look like Abraham Lincoln trying to convince the nation to end the Civil War. But what he's really doing is what married couples the world over do — persuading his partner to do something that goes against her better judgment. "I'll just be gone for a few hours. Just me and the guys going for a beer." "It won't cost much. Really. I promise." "It was only a small dent. I'm sure the insurance will cover it."

In this case, John is trying to make me believe that it really would be easy to have "a few friends" stop by on New Year's weekend, while, in fact, he is tricking me into having a party (two days after we get home from vacation) that he knows I will pour my heart and soul into.

The trick works. We send out invitations just before we leave for the holidays. I will be so relaxed that I'll barely think about this event while we're away. We will come home, no anxiety, and the party will just spontaneously happen. (This is John's train of thought — not mine.)

I try to be cool. I try to be calm. After all, I wrote a book years ago called Relax, Company's Coming! I earn a living teaching others how to be confident when they throw a party. I've built a career teaching the gospel that perfection is not the goal. Enjoying the company of friends and family is what it's all about. I believe this. I really do.

What really happened? We went away. We relaxed and forgot about day-to-day life. We chilled — big time. And then we came home and turned on the computer and there were many, many RSVPs. Our little soiree had turned into a major neighborhood event. Close to seventy-five people told us they were coming. "We are so excited," they wrote. "Can't wait to eat your food — we'll try to bring something." Try? This was a critical part of John's argument. "Make it a pot luck. Then all we have to do is get some champagne and drinks and set out some cheese *and stuff* and it will happen."

You know that book called *Men Are From Mars, Women Are From Venus* or some such nonsense? Well it's times like these, when John says inane things like "All we have to do is get some cheese and drinks and *it will happen*" that I really believe in pop-psych literature.

We get home, and I start cooking. There's spinach from the winter farmer's market and some fresh ricotta, so I make a pastry and fill it with the spinach and ricotta sprinkled heavily with freshly ground nutmeg. I defrost the fresh ham, which was part of a locally raised pig I bought in the early fall, and place it in a spicy brine overnight, before roasting it the next day with a rum-based glaze. I buy some cheeses (one point for John for being technically correct about the menu). And to go with them I make pumpkin seed-rosemary-bacon brittle (my latest obsession). Then I bake a cranberry cheesecake in case no one brings dessert. What if no one brings anything? Maybe I should make a pecan tart, or pistachio-chocolate biscotti. Those little Indian-spiced lamb meatballs with yogurt would be good, or what about a white bean dish (beans being a traditional symbol of good luck for the New Year)? Yes, beans would be good. A sweet potato gratin with the ham sounds fabulous, and maybe a . . .

"POT LUCK!" screams John. "You don't have to make everything. Keep it simple. The whole point is that everyone will bring food. Just chill."

*Chill!* It's starting to snow and turn gray. There's the chill. But in here I am baking and simmering. The friends will come. We will hug and toast. We will eat good food and have a good time. I will have a good time. John will be relaxed and it will all work out the way he says it will. I know it will. But maybe I should make another spinach tart just in case . . .

The night before the party: The forecast is for freezing rain and snow. No one will come. I have all this food. Oh, well. I am chill.

The day of the party: The roasted ham looks and smells amazing; the white beans are so tender, having marinated all night in fresh shredded basil and rich, green olive oil. The snow is picking up and the forecast is for high winds and up to eighteen inches of snow. Guests are bailing out, cancellation phone calls and emails coming in by the handful. I am still chill.

The day after the party: Truth? It was huge fun. Many people floated in and out of here, bringing beautiful food and great bottles of wine. We laughed hard and saw many old friends. People looked happy. I'm so exhausted I feel like a truck ran over me. Was it worth it? Definitely. Was I calm? Absolutely. Will I do it again next year? Well that's still up in the air, but John was right (he earns another point, this time for making a persuasive argument). *It was fun.* Ending one year and starting a new one with people you love, good food, and wine . . . well that's not bad! And I'm pretty sure there was enough food. Yeah, pretty sure.

# Spinach, Feta, *and* Ricotta Tart *with* Nutmeg

Make the pastry a day or several hours ahead of time to let it chill sufficiently. The tart is best served warm from the oven, but will hold up overnight and can be reheated in a low (250 degree) oven until just warm. You'll need a tart pan (11 x 8 inches) with a removable bottom.

*Serves 6*

### For the pastry:

1½ cups flour
salt
⅛ teaspoon ground nutmeg
1½ sticks unsalted butter, well chilled and cut into small pieces
½ cup ice cold water

### For the tart:

1½ tablespoons olive oil
4 packed cups baby spinach or fresh spinach (stem larger spinach leaves)
¼ teaspoon ground nutmeg
salt and freshly ground black pepper to taste
1 cup ricotta cheese or sour cream
⅓ cup heavy cream
2 eggs
1 cup crumbled feta cheese

To make the pastry, whirl the flour, salt, and nutmeg in the container of a food processor. Add the butter and pulse about 15 times, or until the butter in the mixture looks like coarse cornmeal. With the motor running, add only enough of the ice water so that the dough just starts to hold together and pull away from the sides of the food processor bowl.

Alternately, mix the flour, salt, and nutmeg in a large bowl. Add the butter and, using your fingers or a pastry blender, blend it into the flour so that the mixture resembles coarse cornmeal. Make a well in the center of the mixture and add enough of the ice water to make the dough just come together.

Wrap the dough in a large piece of aluminum foil, bunching the dough up into a ball, and chill for at least 1½ hours or overnight.

Working on a well-floured surface, roll out the dough to fit a tart pan that is 11 x 8 inches. You can also use a round tart pan or a pie plate, but a tart pan with a removable bottom is your best bet. Place the dough into the tart pan and trim off the sides. (You can save any leftover pastry for another pie or tart, or discard.) Place in the refrigerator for at least 30 minutes to chill.

Meanwhile, make the filling in a large skillet: heat the oil over moderately high heat. Add the spinach in batches, stirring well and adding more as it begins to cook down. When all the spinach has been added, sprinkle with half of the nutmeg and season with the salt and pepper. Cook for about 4 minutes, or until soft. Remove from the heat. Place the spinach on a large plate and place another plate of the same size on top and, working over a sink, squeeze out the excess moisture from the spinach, discarding the liquid. If using baby spinach you can leave it whole, but if using large spinach leaves you want to chop it coarsely.

In a large bowl, whisk the ricotta, cream, and eggs. Season with salt, pepper, and the remaining nutmeg. Add the drained spinach and the feta and mix.

Preheat the oven to 400 degrees.

Place the filling inside the chilled crust. Place on a cookie sheet and bake on the middle shelf for 30 minutes. Reduce the temperature to 350 degrees and bake another 15 to 20 minutes, or until the tart puffs up slightly, is a pale golden brown, and a toothpick inserted in the center comes out clean. Remove from the oven and pull off the outside rim of the tart pan.

Serve warm or at room temperature. To reheat, place in a low (250 degree) oven for about 10 minutes.

181

# Pumpkin Seed, Rosemary, *and* Bacon Brittle

I was reviewing John Besh's wonderful book *My New Orleans: The Cookbook* (Andrews McMeel Publishing) and discovered a recipe for pumpkin seed brittle that is scattered over a green salad with bleu cheese. I was intrigued. I tried it and was hooked — a combination of sweet and spicy with meaty pumpkin seeds. But I thought I could take it a step further. I experimented by adding chopped fresh rosemary and loved the way the herb brought out the meaty flavor of the pumpkin seeds. But, what else? Well, the answer to almost everything is bacon. I cooked up a few strips of thick country-style bacon, made another batch of brittle, crumbled in the bacon, and it was exactly what I was looking for. Imagine a savory brittle that is both sweet (from sugar) and hot (from a good sprinkle of cayenne pepper) and earthy (from the rosemary) and chewy (from the pumpkin seeds) and fabulous (from the bacon). I warn you: This stuff is truly addictive. I've made many batches and always crave more. It was a huge hit at our holiday party!

Serve the brittle with cheeses, crumble it up over winter salads (mixed greens with pomegranate seeds and crumbled local goat cheese is an amazing combination), or serve it with wine and cocktails.

> 2 to 3 strips thick country-style bacon
> 1 cup sugar
> 1 teaspoon salt
> 1½ tablespoons fresh rosemary, finely chopped, or 1 tablespoon dried
>     and crumbled
> ½ teaspoon cayenne pepper
> 1 cup pumpkin seeds
> 1 egg white

Cook the bacon over moderate heat in a large skillet until crisp and cooked through, being careful not to let it burn. Drain on paper towels. Crumble the bacon into small (but not tiny) pieces and set aside.

Preheat the oven to 375 degrees. Line a baking or cookie sheet with parchment paper or a silicon mat or aluminum foil.

In a medium bowl, mix the sugar, salt, rosemary, cayenne, bacon pieces, and pumpkin seeds.

In another bowl, whisk the egg white for just a few minutes until it is foamy, *but not stiff*. If you overbeat the egg white, the brittle will puff and have too much air, and will not be crunchy. You only need to beat the egg for a few minutes (I do it by hand with a whisk so I can control it), until it just starts to foam. Fold the egg white into the pumpkin seed mixture.

Place the brittle mixture onto the prepared cookie sheet, spreading it thinly and evenly with a soft spatula. Bake about 25 minutes, or until the brittle is a good golden brown color. Remove and let cool. Separate the brittle into $1^1/_2$–inch pieces.

The brittle will keep, covered, in a cookie tin or a tightly sealed plastic bag, for several days.

### Tip

*You can use 2 or 3 strips of bacon depending on how meaty you want the brittle. I prefer 2 strips, making the bacon a more subtle presence, but if you really love bacon, go for 3 strips.*

# Roasted Ham *with* Orange-Rum Glaze

Orange and rum add a delicious, gooey glaze to a country ham. You can also substitute cranberry or pineapple juice. Look for a really good smoked country ham. The better the quality of your ham, the better the dish will be.

*Serves 10 to 12*

> one (12 to 14 pound) fully cooked, smoked, bone-in country ham
> ¹/₄ cup whole cloves
> 1 cup apple cider without preservatives
> 2 cups orange juice, preferably freshly squeezed or juice with pulp
> 1 cup good-quality rum

Preheat the oven to 350 degrees. Place the ham in a large roasting pan. Using a small sharp knife, make several small slits into the top of the ham (at 2-inch intervals the side with the most fat) and insert a clove into each slit, setting aside about eight cloves. Pour ¹/₂ cup of the apple cider on top of the ham and roast for 30 minutes on the middle shelf.

Meanwhile, prepare the glaze: in a medium saucepan, heat the remaining apple cider, the orange juice, rum, and remaining teaspoon of cloves over high heat. Bring to a boil, reduce the heat to low, and simmer for about 15 minutes, or until the mixture begins to thicken slightly. It should just start to stick to a spoon.

Remove the ham from the oven and pour the glaze on top. Continue roasting the meat until the internal temperature reaches 140 degrees, about 12 minutes per pound. A small sharp knife inserted in the meat should be warm to the touch when withdrawn after 30 seconds. Be sure to baste the ham several times during the roasting, to really coat the meat with the glaze. If the glaze appears to be drying out, add more cider and orange juice to keep it moist.

Remove the ham from the oven and place on a carving board; cover loosely with foil to keep warm. Remove any excess fat from the roasting pan.

Carve the ham into thin slices and serve with the warm glaze from the bottom of the pan spooned on top.

### Tip

*Boneless hams are really popular, but I don't think they have as much flavor. Plus, working with a bone-in ham means you can make soup when the party is over!*

# HELLO DARKNESS, MY OLD FRIEND:
# A CHANUKAH STORY

I t's that time of year. The days are miserably short. I feel like eating dinner at about five o'clock, and by 9 P.M., I'm ready to crawl into a dark hole (otherwise known as my bed). I don't feel depressed (I know it sounds otherwise, but really, honestly, truly, doctor, I'm fine); It's just that when the days are cut short like this, so is my energy. It's no wonder that people all over the world embrace the holidays. They seem to be saying: "Damn the darkness; light the candles, decorate the tree, and let's lift our spirits."

In our family we celebrate a little bit of everything. When my daughters were little, we succumbed and did it all — Chanukah, the menorah, the Christmas tree, Santa, stockings, prime rib of beef, Yorkshire pudding. But now that they are grown and off in the world, we've left the whole Christmas thing behind. Except for stockings. That's the one vestige of my children's holiday traditions that we hold onto. Filling a big old red sock with goodies — both edible and otherwise — is just too much fun to let go.

We will also make potato pancakes — the "official" food of the Festival of Lights — and fry them in hot oil until they develop a gorgeous, crispy, crunchy exterior with a soft, comforting potato interior. We will dip the *latkes* into homemade applesauce *(page 153)*, or sour cream and chives, and spread them with just enough fiery horseradish to make our eyes tear up. We will put a match to the menorah candles and for a few hours, for eight nights in dark December, the world will seem just a bit brighter.

# John's Traditional *Latkes* (Potato Pancakes)

Each year John makes these classic potato pancakes. Use a good, locally grown Maine potato (medium starch) and, if possible, forget about cholesterol and all those other health warning that are so firmly planted in your head. If you get the oil nice and hot (but not burning), the pancakes will be golden brown on the outside and absorb relatively little grease. Serve with sour cream, horseradish, and Roasted Apfelmus (Applesauce) *(page 153)*. The pancakes are also delicious served with smoked trout or salmon and dill sprigs.

*Makes about 16 pancakes; serves 4 to 6*

> 6 medium potatoes, peeled, about 2 pounds
> 1 egg
> ¹/₂ teaspoon sea salt
> freshly ground black pepper
> a generous 1 tablespoon flour
> safflower or canola oil or shortening, for frying
> toppings: applesauce, white horseradish, and sour cream
>     (mixed with minced fresh chives), smoked fish with fresh dill

Using a food processor or a hand-held grater, grate the potatoes finely. Place in a large bowl and let sit 5 minutes. Remove some of the starchy liquid that forms in the bowl.

In a small bowl, whisk the egg. Add the egg to the potatoes and season generously with salt and pepper. Sprinkle on the flour and stir in gently to incorporate all the ingredients.

Add 2 to 3 cups of oil to a large skillet (with at least two-inch-high sides to protect you from hot oil splatter; the oil should come up about an inch) over high heat. To test to see if the oil is hot enough, add a small piece of the grated potato and the oil should sizzle up immediately. If the potato seems to burn, reduce the heat a bit. If it doesn't sizzle right up, let the oil get hotter.

Add a heaping tablespoon of pancake batter to the hot oil. Add several other pancakes, being careful not to crowd the skillet, and cook about three minutes on each side, or until they are golden brown on both sides. Test one (lucky you) and make sure it is hot and cooked through to the middle. Repeat with the remaining batter.

Drain the *latkes* on paper towels or thick paper bags. If you're not serving them right away, keep warm in a low (250 degree) oven. But don't let them sit too long. Serve hot with the toppings listed above.

# Mini Sweet Potato *and* Shallot Pancakes *with* Toppings

This is a twist on traditional *latkes*, or potato pancakes, using sweet potatoes, which are so much less starchy, colorful, and healthier than plain old white ones. I like serving them on a platter with various toppings: a dollop of sour cream on one pancake, another with Roasted Apfelmus (Applesauce) *(page 153)*, mango chutney, and apple chutney. Pick one or use them all.

*Makes 16 two-inch pancakes; serves 4*

> 4 medium sweet potatoes, about 1 1/2 pounds
> 2 medium shallots, peeled
> 2 eggs, whisked
> salt and freshly ground black pepper, to taste
> 1/4 teaspoon freshly grated nutmeg
> 1/4 cup flour, plus 1 tablespoon
> 3 cups vegetable oil
> toppings: sour cream, applesauce, mango chutney, and apple chutney

Using the largest opening on a cheese grater, grate the potatoes into a large bowl. Grate the shallots on the same large opening and mix with the potatoes. Add the eggs, salt, pepper, nutmeg, and flour and stir well to fully incorporate all the ingredients.

Preheat the oven to 300 degrees.

In a large heavy skillet, heat the oil over high heat. The oil should be at least 1-inch thick. Let the oil get really hot. To test, add a small piece of grated potato — the oil should sizzle right up. Make a pancake from about 2 heaping tablespoons of batter, forming it into a pancake about 2 inches wide. Add the pancakes to the hot oil, being careful not to overcrowd the skillet. Cook for 2 minutes. Reduce the heat slightly and, using a slotted spoon, gently flip the pancake over. Cook for another 2 minutes. Drain on paper towels. Repeat with the remaining batter. You can keep the drained, cooked pancakes warm on a cookie sheet in the preheated oven for 5 to 10 minutes.

Serve hot with any or all of the toppings listed above.

## Variations:

• Use carrots instead of sweet potatoes and add a pinch of ground ginger instead of nutmeg. Serve with thick Greek-style yogurt.

• Add 1/4 cup minced chives or cilantro to the pancake batter and add very thinly sliced scallions instead of shallots.

187

# MENUS ≋

## Dinner by the Fire

◆ Maine Shrimp, Haddock, and Jerusalem Artichoke Winter Chowder, *pages 24–25*

◆ Roasted Root Vegetable Salad with Basil Vinaigrette and Crumbled Feta, *page 34*

◆ Roasted Garlic Bread, *page 176*

◆ Triple Chocolate and Macadamia Nut Biscotti, *pages 38–39*

## Weeknight Winter Dinner

◆ Leek, Potato, and Sharp Cheddar Cheese Soup with Chive-Walnut-Cheddar Swirl, *pages 166–167*

◆ Spinach, Feta, and Ricotta Tart with Nutmeg, *pages 180–181*

◆ Winter Greens with Pumpkin Seed, Rosemary, and Bacon Brittle, *pages 182–183*

## Snow-Day Dinner

◆ Chicken Stew with Bacon, Baby Onions, and Crimini Mushrooms, *pages 22–23*

◆ Parsleyed Potatoes, *page 21*

◆ Winter Salad of Balsamic-Glazed Turnips and Baby Greens, *page 31*

◆ Roasted *Apfelmus* (Applesauce), *page 153*

## Soup, Salad, Sweets

◆ Greek-Style Turkey-Lemon Rice Soup, *page 174*

◆ Roasted Wild-Mushroom Soup, *page 150*

◆ Greens with Green Green Goddess Dressing, *page 88*

◆ Maple Cheesecake with Maple-Ginger Crust, *pages 46–47*

## Italian Night

◆ Linguine with Maine Clam Sauce, Ramps, and Garlic, *page 72*

◆ Spaghetti with End-of-the-Season Roasted Tomato Sauce, *page 131*

◆ Angry Lobster, *pages 122–123*

◆ Grilled Pizza with Grilled Zucchini, Tomato, and Pesto, *pages 94–95*

◆ Triple Chocolate and Macadamia Nut Biscotti, *pages 38–39*

---

## Valentine's Dinner or Dinner for Two Anytime

◆ Maine Crab Cakes, *page 32*

◆ Sautéed Scallops with Parsnip Puree, *pages 52–53*

◆ Roasted Parsnips and Carrots with Maple Glaze, *page 51*

◆ Creamed Spinach with Yogurt and Nutmeg, *page 82*

◆ Rich Dark-Chocolate Tart with Maine Sea Salt, *pages 36–37*

---

## Hot Summer Night

◆ Cold Cucumber Soup with Mint, Dill, and Lemon, *page 109*

◆ Latin-Style Lobster Salad, *page 121*

◆ Grilled Swordfish with Sautéed Corn, Tomato, and Basil, *pages 142–143*

◆ Fresh Corn-Cracked, Pepper-Scallion Cornbread, *page 141*

◆ Berry Cobbler, *page 103*

◆ Soda with Wild Maine Blueberry Syrup, *page 137*

## Winter Brunch

- Pan-Fried, Cornmeal-Coated Maine Smelts, *page 18*
- Emma's Spinach and Smoked-Salmon Benedict with Artichoke-Caper-Lemon Butter, *pages 78–79*
- Spiced Parsnip Cupcakes with Maple Cream Cheese Frosting, Toasted Walnuts, and Crystallized Ginger, *pages 54–55*

## Spring Brunch

- Maya's Fruit Salad with Blood Orange Juice and Mint, *page 79*
- Bagels and an Assortment of Herb-Flavored Cream Cheese
- Roasted Spring Asparagus with Orange, Feta Cheese, and Poached Eggs, *page 60*
- Grilled Salmon with Maple Glaze and Sea Salt, *page 48*
- Ginger Shortcakes with Local Strawberries and Lemon Cream, *pages 90–91*
- Wild Maine Blueberry Mimosas, *page 137*

## Summer Brunch

- Maya's Fruit Salad with Blood Orange Juice and Mint, *page 79*
- Herb and Feta Corn Fritters, *page 139*
- Fried Eggs in Olive Oil with Chive Oil Drizzle, *page 59*

## Autumn Apple Brunch

- Baked Spiced Apple-Raisin Pancakes, *page 154*
- Breads with Apple Cider Jelly, *page 157*
- Grilled Gruyère Sandwiches with Maple Caramelized Apples, *page 155*
- Roasted *Apfelmus* (Applesauce), *page 153*
- Warm Apple Cider

## Everyday Breakfast

◆ Fried Eggs in Olive Oil with Fresh Chive Oil Drizzle, *page 59*

◆ Granola, *page 108*

◆ Fresh Fruit

---

## Family Dinner #1

◆ Four-Cheese Macaroni with Thyme-Parmesan Crust, *pages 164–165*

◆ Cucumber and Greens Salad with Green Green Goddess Dressing, *page 88*

◆ Roasted Parsnips and Carrots with Maple Glaze, *page 51*

◆ Roasted Applesauce and Cookies, *page 153*

---

## Family Dinner #2

◆ Roast Chicken with Lemon, Rosemary, and Garlic, *page 80*

◆ Roast Pork with Apples and Pears, *page 168*

◆ Garlic Mashed Potatoes, *page 81*

◆ Fresh Corn-Cracked, Pepper-Scallion Cornbread, *page 141*

◆ Salad

◆ Spiced Parsnip Cupcakes with Maple Cream Cheese Frosting, Toasted Walnuts, and Crystallized Ginger, *pages 54–55*

---

## It's Spring! Dinner

◆ First Harvest Pea and Lettuce Soup, *pages 88–89*

◆ Sautéed Scallops with Parsnip Puree, *pages 52–53*

◆ First Salad, *page 86*

◆ Ginger Shortcakes with Local Strawberries and Lemon Cream, *pages 90–91*

## Early Summer Seafood Party

◆ Lobster and Corn Chowder, *page 120*

◆ Grilled Swordfish with Olive-Lemon-Scallion Topping, *page 102*

◆ Lobster and Mango Salad, *page 126*

◆ Fresh Corn-Cracked, Pepper-Scallion Cornbread, *page 141*

◆ Wild Maine Blueberry Soda, *page 137*

◆ Best Blueberry Pie, *pages 104–105*

## First Night to Eat Outdoors

◆ Grilled Pizza, *pages 94–95*

◆ Grilled Pork Chops with Grilled Rhubarb, *page 93*

◆ Fillet of Sole with Slivered Almonds, Capers, and Whole Lemon Slices, *page 101*

◆ First Salad with Basic French-Style Vinaigrette, *page 87*

◆ Meringue Cake with Vanilla Whipped Cream and Mixed Fruit, *pages 62–63*

193

## Holiday Feast

◆ Grilled Turkey, *page 171*

◆ Cranberry Sauce with Orange, Ginger, Pineapple, and Pecans, *page 172*

◆ Garlic Mashed Potatoes, *page 81*

◆ Creamed Spinach with Yogurt and Nutmeg, *page 82*

◆ Roasted Parsnips and Carrots with Maple Glaze, *page 51*

◆ Winter Salad of Balsamic-Glazed Turnips and Baby Greens, *page 31*

◆ Maple Cheesecake with Maple-Ginger Crust, *pages 46–47*

# RESOURCES ⚙

## January

Fishing on the Cathance River:

For more information on renting smelt camps on the Cathance River in Bowdoinham, contact: Jim's Smelt Camp, 4 Bay Road, Bowdoinham, Maine 04008; 207-666-3049; or email Jim McPherson at smeltchaser@yahoo.com.

## February

Winter Farmers' Markets:

To learn more about finding winter farmers' markets throughout Maine, check out these sites: www.mofga.net/Directories/farmersmarkets/tabid/352/default.aspx; www.farmersmarketonline.com/fm/Maine.htm; www.fruitstands.com/states/maine.htm; snakeroot.net/mffm/index.shtml.

Chocolate: For more information about Byrne & Carlson Chocolates, 121 State Street, Portsmouth, NH 03801 and 60 State Road, Kittery, Maine 03904; 888-559-9778 or info@bryneandcarlson.com; or orders@bryneandcarlson.com.

For more information about Maine sea salt, contact Maine Sea Salt Company, 11 Church Lane, Marshfield, Maine 04654; 207-255-3310 or www.maineseasalt.com.

## March

Maple Syrup:

For more information about maple syrup and buying Maine maple syrup, check out www.mainemapleproducers.com and www.mofga.org. You can also find a map of Maine sugarhouses that particpate in Maine Maple Sunday, a great day celebrating Maine maple syrup that takes place in late March.

## April

Chickens:

We bought our baby chicks through the mail from Murray McMurray Hatchery. It sells dozens of interesting varieties: www.mcmurrayhatchery.com/index.html. 191 Closz Drive, P.O. Box 458, Webster City, Iowa 50595; 515-832-3280 or 800-456-3280.

Cooperative Extension puts out several useful pamphlets on raising chicks. They can also help you find someone who raises chickens in your area: extension.umaine.edu/publications/2072e.

Heritage Foods USA sells many interesting varieties of chickens (for roasting, not live birds): www.heritagefoodsusa.com/index.html.

## September

Canning:
There are several good sites that can help you learn more about the basics and technical aspects of canning:

Ball jars has informational videos and more:
www.freshpreserving.com/pages/step_by_step_low_acid_foods/35.php.
The USDA site has all sorts of good information about safety tips:
www.uga.edu/nchfp/publications/publications_usda.html.

## October

Mushrooms:
Rick Tibbets sells mushrooms and wild forest vegetables to some of the top chefs in Portland. You can find his "wild" foods in season at Hugo's, Cinque Terra, and the Corner Room. For more information, contact the Mushroom Man at mushroomman9@yahoo.com.

Apples:
For information about finding an apple orchard near you contact the Maine Department of Agriculture, Food and Rural Resources, 28 State House Station, Augusta, ME 04333-0028, and ask for a copy of their publication *Finding Maine Food and Farms*.
To learn more about local apple orchards in Maine check out www.maineapples.org/orchards.html.

## November

Giving Back:
To learn more about the Let's Move initiative and see what schools in your area are involved, check out:
healthymeals.nal.usda.gov/nal_display/index.php?tax_level=1&info_center=14&tax_subject=225.

To find out about helping out in a local soup kitchen, contact your local church or synagogue.

Here are a few soup kitchens/food pantries in Maine that are always looking for help:
www.preblestreet.org/soup_kitchens.php
Good Shepherd Food-Bank, 3121 Hotel Road,
P.O. Box 1807, Auburn, Maine 04211-1807;
207-782-3554; gsfb.org
www.waysidesoupkitchen.org/

Share Our Strength (SOS) is a national organization committed to wiping our childhood hunger. I have been involved with the Maine chapter of SOS. Every year SOS throws a huge gala event with many of the state's top chefs. To learn more about the Taste of the Nation event and getting involved in helping wipe out childhood hunger in Maine, check out:
www.strength.org/portlandme.

# RECIPE INDEX ✺